T0196098

FREE to a GOOD HOME

DAVID F. LAMBERT

ARCHWAY
PUBLISHING

Archway Publishing books may be ordered through booksellers or by contacting:

Archway Publishing
1663 Liberty Drive
Bloomington, IN 47403
www.archwaypublishing.com
844-669-3957

Because of the dynamic nature of the Internet, any web addresses or links contained in
this book may have changed since publication and may no longer be valid. The views
expressed in this work are solely those of the author and do not necessarily reflect the
views of the publisher, and the publisher hereby disclaims any responsibility for them.

Any people depicted in stock imagery provided by Getty Images are
models, and such images are being used for illustrative purposes only.
Certain stock imagery © Getty Images.

Interior Image Credit: C.A. Hoffman

ISBN: 978-1-6657-0237-9 (sc)
ISBN: 978-1-6657-0236-2 (hc)
ISBN: 978-1-6657-0238-6 (e)

Library of Congress Control Number: 2021902037

Print information available on the last page.

Archway Publishing rev. date: 03/29/2021

INTRODUCTION

I'D LIKE TO TELL YOU ABOUT A SMALL FARM IN SOUTHEAST-
ern New Hampshire. My voice isn't as strong as it used to be,
so if you folks in the back have trouble hearing me, let me
know, and I'll try to speak a little louder. The cast of characters
includes Janet, my wife and enabler; Maggie, the principal animal and subject of the story; Thatcher, a retiring sophisticate
and cautious companion of the main character; Tucker, 150
pounds of wandering fool; and Pete, the killer cat. I'll fill in
details about these characters and others as we go along.

For an assortment of reasons, I'm going to ask you not to
touch the animals. Please avoid touching Maggie or letting
Maggie come near you. Be assured that only moments before
she came to join us, she was chasing frogs in the swamp. Then
she would have added some substance to her thick, brown,
slimy, wet coat when she displaced several cubic yards of New
Hampshire soil as she enlarged an already large woodchuck
hole, encouraging the resident family to move on to the next
small farm, there to dine on carrot tops and young, tender lettuce. In addition to this mud mixture, swamp water, and fine,
sandy loam, there could be any manner of foreign substances
embedded in there—sticks, leaves, tree branches, porcupine
quills, and items too various to mention.

You may have the opportunity to touch Thatcher. He's shy and will find a quiet place to take a nap. You will not have the opportunity to touch Tucker because we can't be entirely sure of Tucker's whereabouts. We seldom know where Tucker is unless he's asleep on the couch or eating a giant dish of dog food. If not there, he could be in the next county. Tucker likes to travel.

Do not—I repeat, *do not*—go near or attempt in any way to reach out to touch the cute black-and-white cat! Nothing good ever comes of being nice to the animal. He may be cute, but he is not nice, and my hands display the scar tissue to prove it.

Janet is my life's traveling companion. This has two connotations. One is that we travel together—and we have, to many common and many exotic places. We also travel effortlessly through life together. Janet carries the greater burden these days, and for that, I'm sorry. Life isn't always fair, but it's always life.

My story, along with other people and other animals, is included, but these are the main characters, so we'll start with them.

All stories, as do all lives, contain a dab of fiction, or a truth distorted a little by the storyteller's feeble attempt to introduce a character or plot. It's a bit of fiction that the Aquilina family, dating back several generations, held to a number of proverbial truths, and Chief Michael Aquilina heard the sweet echo of his mother's voice reminding him that bad luck can be brought about by uttering three curses. Nothing required the curses be of a specified topic, or even related—just three curses. Thus ends the fictional part of my story, for it is not fiction that as a consequence of his muttering, "Damn dog! Damn swamp!

Damn Dave!" when he stepped from firm ground into one of the many hidden, lowland depressions, his leather boots, nicely polished when he left home that morning, were over-topped by about a pint of cold, muddy swamp water. The event registered on the pain scale somewhere between a barked shin and a toothache, but it soured his attitude toward the dog and its owner by one more resounding click, like falling tumblers on the big, brass lock on the door of the animal pound. Dave had to learn the concept of the leash law, and Maggie had to be licensed and not allowed to wander.

Mike last saw Maggie when she left the paved road and charged into the timber swamp behind the Universalist church in pursuit of … who knows what or who, and there she re-mained. He traced her movement through evening air so thick with drizzle and fog that her sounds—distant barking, nearer splashing—had substance, like an object that he could hold in his hand. It came from here, then there. Near the church, from the town park, then the Schweitzer farm. She traveled in a great arc, from south to north, then toward the east.

Twice, when she seemed most distant, he was startled by a large animal crashing through the trees and brush just a few yards from where he was standing. Could be a moose, could be a deer … could be that damn dog. He shone his flashlight toward the sound but saw nothing, just the interwoven abatis of decaying clusters of swamp alder, spreading at their tops and bound at the roots to mimic an outsized arrangement of ugly, desiccated cut flowers or a giant game of pick-up-sticks; either could delay and confuse the most experienced swamp runner.

Mike Aquilina was wet, cold, and tired of trying to catch Dave Lambert's dog. His retreat was eased by following a staggered path of small islands where stubborn, stunted pine trees struggled to survive on wheelbarrow-sized dollops of New Hampshire loam. At least they gave him an alternate route that kept his boots from completely filling with swamp water. A half hour of stepping from Lilliputian island to island returned him eventually to his car, parked near the old brick school at the end of Moulton Ridge Road. The bright beam of his military-style flashlight was returned by the two un-blinking, bright eyes of the enormous, mud-encrusted, drip-ping wet, happily panting, unrepentant dog—lolling tongue, waving like a high school pennant. Leaning against the vehi-cle, she had applied a fresh smear of mud on the door of the car, obscuring some of the painted letters: Kensington, New Hampshire Police Department.

Chief Aquilina filled his lungs to clear body and mind, then sat against the hood of the car and focused on the water in his left boot as it sloshed between his toes, and the wet sock that was curled in a sodden ball where his toes were sup-posed to be. Then to the dog he said, "No ride home tonight, Maggie." He opened the back door of the car, and without hesitation, the dog bounded onto the seat, dripping water and mud onto the vinyl seat cover. "I'm taking you somewhere else. Somewhere that neither you nor Dave are going to like, but he has to become a member in good standing of the next century. I know it's a struggle, but … well, he has to learn that Kensington has a leash law." Maggie leaned forward from the back seat and rested her muddy muzzle on Mike's shoulder as he pulled onto the road and started toward Bob Marston's small farm that served as the dog pound.

The animal wasn't bad. To the contrary, she was a good dog. The problem rested with the dog's owner, who couldn't accept that it was the 1990s, not the 1930s. He couldn't accept that farm vehicles, no matter the age, had to be registered before they could be driven on the road; that a farm truck required state safety inspection; and that Kensington, New Hampshire, had a leash law.

Dave responded, "Do you mean I got to keep my dog tied up? That I got to keep her on a leash? How's she going to control the woodchuck and raccoon population while on a leash?"

Less than a week prior, the chief had issued the warning to Dave. "You've got to keep your dog restrained. She can't run all over town. Do something about it, Dave, or I will."

VERSE 1

FREE TO A GOOD HOME. THE CYNIC IN ME BELIEVES THAT nothing is free, but I'm enough of a romantic to believe that at times, everything is free. Maggie was named because of Margaret Thatcher. We already had a dog named Thatcher, and Janet couldn't resist naming the six-month-old, sixty-five-pound, "free to a good home" female puppy of indeterminate breeding Margaret. We mostly called her Maggie and sometimes Margaret S. Dog. She would respond to any of these names if she considered it to be in her best interest and respond to none of them if not.

I don't remember exactly when Maggie joined us. It was probably the year of a presidential primary. It always is. Here in New Hampshire, the Live Free or Die state with our first-in-the-nation primary, we're pandered to most years by a host of hopefuls, all determined to be the leader of the free world. There's that word *free* again. If the candidates aren't here, they're either just arriving or just departing. It's kind of like a cold; you're either getting it, have it, or are recovering, and the symptoms can be equally as noxious. Maggie kept us in a similar realm of anticipation, waiting for the next oversized, mud-caked foot to fall. Where and when ... It was always where and when. She came, was here, and hasn't completely left, although it's been a number of years since I found her one morning, next to her water bowl, lying lifeless on the kitchen floor.

Maggie's heritage was maybe collie and Great Pyrenees; we were never sure. Janet selected her by chance from the remnants of a litter of outsized puppies. The transaction was overseen by the owner's kids, who knew nothing of the dog's lineage. They told my wife that they wanted to keep the puppies, but the resulting parental filibuster carried the day, so she assured them that we would provide a good home, and the deal was sealed. I said that Janet selected the dog by chance, but she picks out her animals using her own procedure for legislating decisions. Not unlike addressing a joint session of Congress, she makes a statement to the assembled animals (pigs, sheep, kittens, and in this case dogs). "Blink your eyes if you want to go home with me." Or "Rub your nose on the fence if you want to go home with me." Or maybe "Stick out your tongue," "Lick my hand," "Eat a blade of grass," or whatever, but the operative phrase is of course "if you want to go home with me." I don't know what she said to the litter of puppies, but whatever it was, Maggie did it.

Maggie had the pastel-honey and white color and the soft face of a collie and the massive body and huge feet of a Great Pyrenees, and in time, we started to believe that her intelligence bordered on human—a pretty bright human at that. While with us, she performed sleight of hand (paw) feats of strength, comedy, tragedy, larceny, murder, and yes, on a couple of occasions, magic. She had traits of Tony Soprano, Houdini, Lazarus, and Gandhi. She could be as gentle as a flower petal and as savage as a wolverine. She could rescue a chicken from a fox in the morning and, in her enthusiasm, dispatch the same chicken in the afternoon. She could disappear like Bernie Sanders does from the political scene and reappear days later like, well, Bernie Sanders reappearing on the political scene. One of my keenest memories of Maggie was of her lying in front of the old, polished, Glenwood wood-burning range in our kitchen with our two-year-old grandson, Cameron, stretched on her back as though she were a rug. They were both nearly asleep. Children were as safe with her as with their own parents—and certainly safer than with their often-haphazard grandfather.

This is a song about Maggie—more accurately, a ballad. No, there are no musical notes, and the lyrics as such don't rhyme. Maybe some rhyme but to a very lesser degree and with little intention. She was as unusual to her species as Einstein was to ours. For the ten years or so that she graced us with her life, we were treated to a continuous series of antics and pranks, deeds and misdeeds that sweetened our lives like clover honey. I've spent my lifetime with dogs. Since my first memories, too many years ago, there has been a dog in my life, not just living there but entwined with my life like a rampant vine of bittersweet. They are important to me. I remember them all with an admiration born of companionship and friendship. Each one is vivid in my memory, even if they were with us but a few months, like Bandit, a black Lab who looked for a woodchuck in every football and found joy in every frisbee. Our own Sir Edmond Hillary was a mutt named Lucky who, for twenty years, scrambled to the top of every load—cord wood, hay, fruit, or pickles—because it was there. Lady was a big, beautiful, regal, golden-throated, and witheringly gun-shy Redbone hound who preferred our sedate, open, and hunter-free fields to the periodically exploding woods. She was willing to forgive the rare backfire of an aged tractor.

A flame could not warm me more than the memory of all my dogs, but Maggie's life with us was more than her sharing a few short years; it was a fateful union. It was a time filled with more laughter and tears than our cups of enjoyment could contain. It's taken these several years for me to piece together the entirety of our shared experience, and still I'm certain, no matter how hard I try or how many carefully chosen words I use, I'll fall short by a good measure of painting a finished portrait of Maggie and our time with her. Of course, everyone's dog is special and deserving of volumes—that's not to be denied—but not every dog is part magician, part diplomat, part explorer, part hunter, and part clown. Then again, ask their people. Maybe they are.

VERSE 2

Our posturing presidential candidates present to us their attributes—their defining characteristics—and we're invited to admire their strength, cleverness, and slight of character. If you live in New Hampshire, you have to be careful to avoid them. They're like ice in the winter; it's very slick and slippery, and there's plenty of it. If you haven't met a candidate, you must really keep to yourself. You might border on being a recluse. A monastic ascetic couldn't elude one. Depending on the season, there's usually a contender at every street corner in Exeter and two at the bandstand. And if you have the need to go to Portsmouth or Manchester, you'd better lock your car when you park, or it may have a candidate sitting in it, looking for your vote, by the time you get back.

New Hampshire's first-in-the-nation presidential primary has been with us since 1920. The distinction of being first is important to our state for a number of reasons, not the least of which is monetary. These folks spend a lot of money in their pursuit of the presidency; advertising media, transportation companies, lodging facilities, restaurants, and many others share a slice of the political pie. New Hampshire is easy picking for the candidates. There are but a few densely populated areas in the state, so like a good crop of tomatoes, it's most efficient if you harvest from the healthiest, best-producing plants first. Then you can turn your attention to the ones scattered around the field. For the citizens of New Hampshire, it's an opportunity to meet and maybe even shake the hand of the person who will be our next president. At that time, during our primary season, we don't know who that person is, but the chances are very good that you'll meet him or her if you attend a few political gatherings.

I took a stunning series of photographs of candidate Barack Obama employing the latest in flip phone technology. Janet and I watched him speak to a gathering at Exeter High School, and as the auditorium emptied at the end of his speech, I joined a small crowd gathered to ask questions of the candidate. With each step I took closer to the front of the group, I lifted my phone over my head and took another picture of Senator Obama standing before the group, each photograph a little closer and a little clearer. I might add that as I closed the gap between me, flip phone held aloft, and the future president, who ignored me, I did not go unnoticed by a cluster of a few people who spoke surreptitiously into the lapels of their jackets. The candidate excused himself and left the remainder of us and the gymnasium well before I reached the front of the line, but I wasn't disappointed. I didn't have a question to ask anyway, and I had my photos. I met Janet and some friends outside, but when I proudly displayed my pictures of the candidate, I learned that it was necessary to push a Save button on my phone after each photo taken before going on to the next. All of my excellent photographs had gone to the land of unsaved photos, there to quietly reside with all my other shots not saved.

We live on a pretty typical New Hampshire farm where we grow vegetables and small fruit. The soil is characteristically stony, enough to make tilling a challenge but with adequate fertility to allow our crops some decent yields. Most all the fields on a New England farm slope or roll a little, and ours are no exception. We're living where the last Ice Age terminated twenty thousand or so years ago. The glacier pushed the earth's surface up into a pile that is now mountains, but when the ice melted, it left for our benefit graceful, fertile hillocks of soil just tall enough to allow a stroll to the top, where you can share the vantage point of a giant or a very tall NBA player. This is surrounded by and divided with handsome rubble stone walls. Leave it to the New England farmer, who, centuries ago, when he first settled this land, joined two of his needs with one elegant solution. He moved the stones that littered his fields and impeded his tilling to the edges of the field to create a wall that kept his animals in and his neighbors out. Never has anyone better described a stone wall and its physical and social significance than Robert Frost in "Mending Wall." It should be required reading for all residents of New Hampshire's rural towns. Over time, a rounded, nondescript lump of granite becomes weathered by the elements, grayed with lichen, and nestled with his fellow lumps to create a beautiful, twisting stone tendon that helps hold our state together in body and in spirit. New Hampshire is called the Granite State; it should be called the Small Pieces of Granite Lined up in a Row State. On second thought, Granite State rolls off the tongue a little better.

Call it as you will, good fences make good neighbors. Over the past two hundred fifty years, our farm has been home to cows, sheep, horses, mules, pigs, chickens, turkeys, geese, dogs, cats, and maybe goats, though I've never seen a goat raised here. If Janet had her way, there would be donkeys and llamas added to the catalog. Rocks are our first crop. Every spring, we trudge across the plowed fields, harvesting those pushed up by the winter frost, but the remaining list can include apples, pears, peaches, plums, cherries, red, black and blueberries, strawberries, and any vegetable that will grow in this climate. One season, I even had a nice crop of Spanish peanuts. I have to include brussels sprouts just to see my granddaughter squirm.

> I crave beyond the slightest doubt
> The vegetable called brussels sprout.
> They look like cabbage but petite
> And are the very best to eat.
> I think they taste very good.
> Clemie thinks they taste like wood.

I believe the flavor rapturous.
Clemie's sure they're aliens after us.
I'm so happy when I'm able
To see brussels sprouts upon the table.
Clemie passes them politely,
Though she thinks them quite unsightly.

My parents milked about forty cows here, and George Weare, the farmer who sold them the farm in 1946, had fifty or more fruit trees. The fruit trees were removed to make way for milk cows, and eventually the dairy herd went to New York state with my sister and her husband, where the fields were larger and development smaller, and that's when Janet and I introduced a variety of vegetables and small fruit.

Of course, I can't ignore that one crop needed to feed the great political appetite—the primary vote. Our farm joins the rest of the state every four years to winnow lesser candidates from the field and eventually refine the harvest to a couple of the hardiest remnants. The primary election process isn't that different from raising vegetables. You broadcast some seed, you incorporate abundant natural fertilizer, you pray for inclement weather (candidates actually pray for their opponent to have inclement weather), and with some luck and a lot of sun, you harvest a bountiful crop.

There is a satisfaction in cutting brush. It's akin to housecleaning. Janet does housecleaning occasionally. I don't mean that she cleans the house occasionally. I couldn't write this, knowing she'd read it and say that she cleans house only occasionally. I'm not a masochist. I don't mean vacuuming up the dog hair that blooms on the hand-braided rugs or mopping muddy footprints off the old pine floors. The kind of housecleaning I'm referring to includes at least one trash can or several generous trash bags. I mean throwing away at least half the detritus in a closet or making a substantial path through the family anthology collected in the attic—enough path to open a window for the summer.

It feels good to cut brush. It's cleaning; it's restoring order; it's managing the unmanaged. Our past president, W, liked cutting brush on his Texas ranch; though unlike me, he usually had a press contingent watching. That must be an odd state of affairs, one person sawing or hacking or lopping. I do all three. I don't know about the president. Anyway, one person is raising a prodigious sweat while a group of people armed with notebooks, pencils, BlackBerries, cameras, cell phones, and tape recorders watch and comment. They jot down how many swings of an ax the president takes to cut a sapling or video his method for sharpening a chain saw. Does he file into the tooth or away from the tooth? Does he lop saplings close to the ground, or does he leave stump stubble like a two-week beard? I'm sure there are comparative conclusions made with each movement. Does he appear relaxed and happy, inferring that this is his way of unwinding? His R&R? Or is he petulant and ill-tempered, thrashing in his behavior? Is that small tree he's slashing at, trying to subdue with his ax, a proxy for the president of Russia or maybe the Speaker of the House? Does he imagine a stubborn sapling that he struggles to defeat with his brush cutters to be his press party?

When we had milking cows on our farm, my family would place a fence straddling the stone wall, and the cows, never interested in what's inside the fence, leaned, reached, and extended their supple necks to eat the brush, poison ivy, bittersweet, small maples, sumac, and anything else that grew along the stone wall before it ever became something resembling brushy growth. Back then, we had classic, pristine, New England stone walls worthy of Robert Frost's poem. Now, woody weeds, unrestrained by hungry cows, proliferate in, around, and between the stones like an invading army of toughened vegetative soldiers needing the discipline of my chain saw and ax.

Like I said, I don't remember the year Maggie joined us, but the season was somewhere between weeding pumpkins and harvesting corn. It was a cloudless, shimmering afternoon when a mantle of sopping heat lay on the farm, and the only thing to do about it was try to ignore it. It was the kind of day you could almost hear the corn grow, and the moist heat made the onions push from the warm soil and get large and sweet. Janet had gone to the beach with Pat, her friend from Keene. Pat, who was visiting for a few days, wanted to go to the beach, as do almost all of our summer visitors. When I was a teenager, the magnetic attraction of the New Hampshire coastline was nearly irresistible, but as an adult, the thought of exposing the upper portion of my body to the radiation of a flaming orb, removed only as far distant as our sun from our planet, while at the same time immersing the lower portion of me in ocean water so cold that it's temperature must be regulated by a large iceberg bobbing out of sight just over the horizon, was not pleasing. In fact, the thought of being french fried on the top and flash frozen on the bottom left me happy to be cutting brush on a stone wall near our blueberry bushes.

I shut off the chain saw momentarily to wipe the sweat from my glasses, and I looked up to see a dog pulling my adult daughter toward me on a leash so forcefully that Kelly looked like a rag doll pulled on a string by an excited child. The dog's enormous, flailing, oncoming, dinner-plate feet announced her distinguishing quality—exuberance. Maggie never did anything in half measure. That day, she nearly knocked me down in greeting. Standing on her back feet, her front paws didn't reach my shoulders yet, though in time, they would. Kelly was living in Exeter then, and I thought it was nice that she had this cute, robust dog that she brought by for us to see.

Kelly is a dog person. I didn't think she needed to add to her dog collection, but I did say she was an adult, and though our children are always our children, they do eventually become adults, and we shouldn't question their purposes. Anyway, I thought it was Kelly's dog. I didn't know that it was my wife, urged on by our suddenly disinterested friend, who had succumbed to those eager brown eyes behind the "Free to a good home" sign near the beach in Rye. "Meet your new dog, Dad. Mom wants to name her Margaret," Kelly said. Did Margaret want to be leader of the free world? Maybe.

Maggie sniffed her new surroundings like a … well, like a happy puppy and took a good roll in some poison ivy. Janet can't walk past poison ivy without getting a rash. Still, I had only an inkling of where this situation was going. I don't know who was happier, Kelly with a new puppy that her parents could take responsibility for or Maggie with a new family that she could … She could what? We would all soon find out.

After a day or two, when I regained speech and reason, Janet and I started to discuss how best to *train* our new *pet*. At the time, I thought the two words *train* and *pet* applied to the dog. We learned quickly that Maggie was not a pet, and the training was for us, not her. Fifty years of a variety of farm dogs had me prepared for an animal obedient to man that provided companionship, acted as a greeting party—"Hi, welcome to Walmart"—did small menial tasks, maybe a trick or two, performed a little guard duty, kept some of the raccoons out of the corn, and in general made one's life a tad easier and more comfortable. I wasn't ready for Maggie. This made me more appreciative of our democracy. We have a long parade of presidential candidates who march through our state, and it gives us an opportunity to interview them and make a choice, not have a choice thrust upon us.

Maggie demanded human attention as withered plants demand water. If she caught you looking in her direction, she thought it meant, "Golly, Mags, I'm your best friend, and I want you to put your paws on my shoulders. I want to rough your coat. I want to feed you anything edible on the kitchen counter. I want to be inseparable from you for life." If I scolded her, and in her early years it was often, she'd run into the house, bolt halfway up the front stairs, turn around awkwardly on the narrow pulpit stairway, sit on one tread, put her front paws on several treads lower, and, in a manner I can't adequately describe, flatten her perpetually cocked ears, squint her eyes, compress her muzzle, and twist her mouth into a ridiculous grimace that Janet described as a catfish with a toothache (who knew that catfish had teeth). Her look always brought me to a stifled laugh, yet I couldn't let her see me even smile. It was interpreted as "All's well. Forgiveness is yours. Go back to doing what you were doing—chasing, wandering, eating, stealing, whatever." This was a form of debate—me with my words and wisdom, she with her guttering look and wisdom. I always thought I won the debate; after all, I am man, and man has reason. In truth, I never won the debate, for I'm only man, and I have only reason.

VERSE 3

Our small farm is located on Moulton Ridge Road, a quiet stretch of crumbling pavement with so little traffic that we've had only trivial concerns with our animals' safety. The chickens peck between the cracks in the macadam, and the cats occasionally sun themselves on the warm black surface to take the chill off a spring day. It's a half mile or so to the heavy traffic on Route 150. Don't get the wrong idea; Route 150 is the road connecting Exeter and Amesbury, not Boston and New York or even Portsmouth and the malls in Kittery for that matter. There are more cars going by in an hour than I'd want going past our farm but not so many that you can't walk across 150 without being pretty sure you'll safely gain the other side. And at night, the volume of passing cars slows to a trickle.

We had Maggie with us only a few weeks when our spit-shined, razor-creased police chief, Mike Aquilina, paid us his first visit regarding the dog. She was on Route 150 at night and was a traffic hazard. When we promised to keep her close to the farm and off 150 for the safety of both motorists and dog, I didn't know how difficult that would be. Chief Aquilina was less friendly after his fourth visit. In fact, he was getting a little gruff, so I decided it would be best to keep Maggie in at night.

I don't know why our farmhouse has so many doors leading outside. There are five. Each, in varying degrees, allows cold air to enter during winter and mosquitoes during summer. They permit occupants of the house to exit to a different part of the farm, and each provides a handy and subtle escape route from salesmen, tax assessors, or Chief Aquilina, who are knocking at another door. If you're in a hurry to get to the mailbox, you'd use the front door. The shortest route to the orchard is out one of the back-porch doors, and the other back-porch door is the quickest way to the barn. Our back door leads to the house from our driveway, so that's the door used the most by our guests. That we have a back-porch door (doors) makes one understand that we have a front-porch door, and that's the door used by our household animals.

Our front-porch door is held closed with a simple spring, and any dog or cat worth their independence can enter or leave the house with ease and without any human help for 365 days a year. I should add here that the modus operandum for opening the door by all animals is to scratch tentatively at the bottom of the door, get it bouncing open enough to get their nose into the opening, and slide through. Maggie lifted herself onto her back legs, gripped the doorknob with her paw, pulled open the door, and dropped her giant frame through the opening. She appeared more human opening the door than I. Anyway, this open arrangement allows our household animals the freedom to come and go pretty much at will. All of our dogs, going back generations of dogs and generations of people for that matter, have spent their days and nights roaming the farm or not roaming as they pleased.

Maggie gave new meaning to roaming. A couple of

years into our Maggie experience, Janet met a woman from Brentwood, a town three towns removed from our farm, who exclaimed, "Maggie! You own Maggie? Why, she's just the nicest dog. She comes by for a treat a couple of times a week."

Janet replied, "Oh no! She goes to Brentwood too?"

Janet and I were out one evening. I don't recall why. Maybe to hear one of our presidential candidates speak. We pretty much keep to the farm, but there's nothing quite as reassuring as having a candidate make you a promise that you know they'll abandon only hours after gaining the power you give them to keep the promise. Anyway, it was probably one of those times. We were driving home from Exeter on Route 150, intending to close up the chicken coop and lock Maggie in for the night, and there, near the old brick school at the end of Moulton Ridge Road, exposed by the pickup's headlights, standing on the center line, was a huge yellow dog, the size of a small deer, stopping traffic, pressing her muzzle against the driver's side window of any car that would stop to pass the evening in man-to-dog conversation. Maybe even making promises she didn't intend to keep.

"Dave!" Janet said, proclaiming an epiphany. "She comes here at night to find company! She wants someone to pay attention to her!" And then Janet made the crucial observation. "She's lonely! When we're not with her, she gets lonely, comes down here, and stops cars to visit with people."

"Dog's don't get lonely," I said. "Besides, Thatcher's at the farm. The cats are there. They're good company." Thatcher was good company; I'm not sure about the cats.

When I opened the pickup door, Maggie climbed over me, her huge feet dropping clods of mud on my clothes, and sat between us, pink tongue extended, hot breath fogging up the windshield. I'd probably have to hose out the truck in the morning, but I certainly couldn't ask her to ride in back; she might get lonely on that half-mile ride home. I could have asked Janet to get in back, but then …

The next day, with a length of rope, I tied Maggie to the big willow in the backyard. A nice place to be tied up if there was one. The spreading tree offered cool shade and a pleasant view of the house and barn in one direction and our small orchard with open fields beyond in another. I placed a fresh pan of water within easy reach and left her a raw beef bone Janet bought at the store. I think I told myself that it was a temporary solution. Maggie would see the error of her ways and would, when next allowed freedom, sensibly stay within the reasonable confines of a one-hundred-fifty-acre farm. After all, farms and dogs were meant to go together—the dog enjoying the large-scale limits of the farm, and the farm enjoying the protection and service of the dog.

Our candidates don't run for the vice presidency, and similarly, Maggie had little intention of being second in command. Instead of quietly lying under the tree and snoozing the day away, within minutes, she chewed through the rope and came to join me planting tomatoes in the garden. There was a warm sun on my back, a throaty pair of cardinals trebling from a maple on the fence line, and I was enjoying the slip of moist soil through my fingers and the rich smell of spring-moistened earth. There is a special relationship between a farmer and his soil. Everything a farmer does relates to the soil on his farm. Some farmers will tell you that the baling wire used to keep worn-out machinery running for one more year is the essence of farming, but it really is the soil. And it is *soil*, not *dirt*. Dirt is what you find under the refrigerator. Soil is the soul of a farm. There is only a vowel difference between *soil* and *soul*—maybe for a reason. To run your hands through it is like holding the stuff of existence itself—the medium that permits life to be. Rocks and weeds are another matter. They are to farming what truth is to a candidate—something that gets in the way of one of life's nearly perfect journeys.

Anyway, Maggie joined me by sweeping in from my blind side, where she artfully dug up a few plants I had carefully planted, then mashed the rest of the new planting into the soil with her whopping feet. She playfully took a tray of new plants in her teeth and shook them free of potting soil, knocked over the five-gallon bucket of trans-plant solution, worked fertilized water and topsoil into mud with the skill of an Sicilian grape stomper, wiped one dripping paw on my relatively clean T-shirt, then ran off through the field to hunt woodchucks, dragging a short length of rope as evidence of her short-lived confinement. Just then, Janet called from the back door of the house that Maggie had freed herself from the rope tied skillfully to the willow tree. I just sat in the mud created by the overturned planting solution and considered platitudes about man's best friend.

Next, accompanied by a small, dark cloud hovering over my usual optimism, I tied Maggie to the willow with a length of light chain that made me as unhappy as it did her. My belief in the symbiotic union of farm and dog was being mightily challenged. Any dog, even a large dog, should be happy with the confines of so much land, not that I expected her to clearly understand the boundaries. After all, she wasn't a surveyor (or the tax assessor), but I thought the expanse of field and woodland would be enough room to roam for any dog. There should be enough squirrels and woodchucks to keep her interest; I knew that there were plenty from my point of view. But nothing was quite enough for Maggie.

After about a week of whining, howling, barking, and straining at the chain, we tried giving her a little freedom, and she responded pretty well. She continued to visit the immediate neighbors but stayed within a reasonable radius of the farm.

A few days later, I was driving the tractor past Rudy Hede's house, our immediate neighbor to the west, and saw Maggie looking out at me through the glass panel from the inside of Rudy's front storm door. I waved, and she wagged but made no attempt to come out of Rudy's house and join me. I wondered if Rudy would like to own Maggie on a permanent basis—have her change parties, so to speak. Then she'd spend some of her time at the farm, and if she strayed to Route 150, Rudy could listen to Chief Aqualina. I think Rudy and Maggie liked the present arrangement.

VERSE 4

Maggie, if she was anywhere near the farm, liked to be with me when I drove the tractor. My father had a rich, deep, baritone voice and enjoyed singing. He sang in the church choir, he sang solos in church, he sang in the plays the Grange Society presented at the Grange Hall, and he sang at many community events held at the town hall. But his greatest, most honored stage was from the seat of his tractor. Whether mowing, raking, baling, plowing, or spreading manure, he sang every song he knew, and there were thousands. He could sing for a week straight and not repeat a chorus or verse. He sang everything from "The Old Rugged Cross" to the bawd of Tin Pan Alley, from show tunes to military marches, from opera to pop tunes (from the early twentieth century—he stopped being interested in pop music with, I think, Elvis). Tractor singing is not directed at a selected audience; it's more a paean from your crop to the heavens. You feel removed from an audience by the slightly muted roar of the tractor engine and by the distance your field keeps you from the rest of humanity. The singer thinks the roar of the tractor engine, like the murk of a spring fog, will mask his voice from critical ears.

The point of this is that I inherited Dad's aspiration for tractor singing, though none of his gifts for tractor singing.

The neighbors suffer the most. They used to listen to Glorious Gus, and now they're treated to Discordant Dave. I have little or no musical ability, or any abilities for that matter. My father had a wonderful voice; my mother played the piano quite well. My sisters are both intelligent and dedicated teachers, and well, then there's me. My mother insisted that I take piano lessons, but after torturing Mrs. Blake, my piano teacher, for a few years, everyone gave up and allowed me to dedicate my life to Little League Baseball, and I became one of the more consistent bench players for the Exeter Red Sox. We kept the piano in the living room, and it's a wonderful conversation piece. "Oh," a visitor will say. "Do you play?" "No" is my reply. End of conversation. But it directs us into other subjects like the price of tractor tires.

Maybe Maggie thought my singing was conversation. Maybe she thought I was talking to her. Who knows? To a dog, the lyrics of "I've Got You under My Skin" might sound like "I sure am glad you've chosen to join me here in the field." "I've got you deep in the heart of me" sounds like "It is my greatest pleasure that you've graced me with your presence." "So deep in my heart you're nearly a part of me" may be interpreted as "As soon as I'm done here, we could go for a swim together in the pond and then chase the chickens." Or it may make as much sense to her as a market report does to anyone other than one selling something in the market. Does anyone but a farmer understand or care about the wholesale cost of a bushel of shell peas in July? Whatever the reason, Maggie liked to be with me in the field. She'd browse around for rabbits and field mice but spent most of her time either walking beside the tractor or finding a central point, maybe on one of those restive hillocks where she could sit or lie and just watch me and perhaps dream, if dogs dream, of a woodchuck to chase or a piping roast to remove from the kitchen counter.

I want to include a brief note about tractors. Some farmers buy new tractors. I know that they do because that's where old tractors—the tractors we have—live their first lives. I have fallen prey to the inviting luxury of the soft, cushioned seat of a new tractor and held the smooth, unchipped steering wheel in my hands. Once, while at the local John Deere dealer (one of my favorite places on the planet), I started the engine of a new John Deere. It was as smooth and quiet as Chief Aquilina's police cruiser, but I turned it off immediately. I was afraid that the siren call of that smooth power would lure me straight into the sales desk, and I'd make a mistake that would take my remaining lifetime to pay off.

A few things I couldn't help but notice about the new tractors. You don't need to jump-start them off the pickup truck each time you use them, or park them on a hill and, when the time comes to start the engine, break inertia a with a superhuman shove against one of those big back tires and, once they're rolling, pop the clutch and pray that you'll have some black smoke drifting from the muffler before gravity is no longer your friend and you'll need to dig deeper into your vast store of old tractor tricks if you want to use the contrary beast before lunch. The new tractor had a key that you simply turned to start it and not two bare wires that you needed to twist together before, with hope in your heart and a silent prayer on your breath, you jammed your foot against the starter pedal to start it. It wasn't necessary to inflate at least one tire before each use. And nestled serenely among the gleaming gauges and levers was a cup holder! A cup holder. What a clever idea! I can never recall holding a cup of any kind while driving a tractor, except maybe a can of oil, but for days after, I dreamed of crossing my field, cradled in the air-conditioned luxury of my new John Deere, with a cup full of—I didn't know what—gently secured in my cup holder.

Our newest tractor was new during the first Reagan administration. Lyndon Johnson was president when our Oliver was manufactured, and we have two from the Eisenhower years and one from the Roosevelt years—actually while Truman served out Roosevelt's last term, so it's not as old as it might sound. Tractors have evolved from the first basic replacements for draft horses to the powerful, efficient machines that are at my John Deere dealer today. The new tractors look nothing like my collection—they have paint on them, for instance—but in their function, they're not much different: they pull an attached load. Our tractor from the Reagan years, a John Deere, is multifunctioned and industrious. It looks more streamlined and polished than my older tractors, although in terms of actual horsepower, it's not exceptionally powerful. The engine starts with cheerful ease, though it has a jar-of-marbles rattle of a diesel engine. It gets more use than the others because it's the most sophisticated, and due to its relative modernity, it's capable of a wide range of tasks. The small, efficient engine is very conservative of fuel. It has a loader attached, so it is useful if I have to tear down that wall (or pile of snow).

The Oliver was built at the beginning of Lyndon Johnson's final term. But for his assassination, it would probably have been at the beginning of Kennedy's second term. It's a workhorse if there ever was one. Big, comfortable to operate (Janet's favorite), powerful, and smooth. We use it for our heavy lifting—plowing, harrowing, and spraying. It uses fuel liberally, so we don't use it for menial tasks. But if you need to integrate white fertilizer with dark soil or see the light at the end of the growing season, the Oliver is the machine to use.

The two tractors from the Eisenhower years are conservatively built and industrious, though for us, their use is quite specific. They are capable of a wider range of utilization than that to which we apply them. One is used almost strictly for cultivating weeds, thereby maintaining straight, evenly spaced, weed-free, and uncontaminated rows of vegetables, and the other, clanking its tank-like tracks and pushing with its bulldozer blade, though it hasn't even run for several years, is used for maintaining a smooth, flat, crisp, well-ordered, almost military appearance to our fields.

The oldest, and my favorite, was built (probably in Dubuque) while Harry was givin' 'em hell! Like me, it's old, slow, loud, unsophisticated, underpowered, and in bad need of a good cleaning. It's as close to ancient history as you can get and still have internal combustion. I have to invent jobs for its use because there's really nothing it can do that any of the other tractors can't do quickly, quietly, and with greater efficiency, but it's dependable and perfect for finishing up after the close of the year and settling the farm to a quiet off season.

When repairing one of our tractors, and repairs are often required, my hands are smeared with the combined color of red rust and grease-impregnated dust and soil (or dust-impregnated grease) the color of night—a permanent stain that often takes a gasoline rinse and days of liberal scrubbing with a stiff brush at the bathroom sink. Death at the hands of my good wife would soon follow if I washed in the kitchen sink. My clothes are another matter. They are permanently stained with a grease, rust, dust, sweat combination that—if nothing else—provides me with some unique color patterns the envy of the tie-dye crowd.

I don't want to wander from my story about Maggie. We were planting strawberries one time—transplanting actually. That's what you do with strawberries; instead of planting a seed, you place a small plant in the soil. Using a machine to transplant is an interesting process. The machine is pulled behind a tractor, with two operators on the transplanter placing young strawberry plants on a tray, where two mechanical, rubber-faced hands take the plant and place it in the ground. It enables two people to do the work of four. It's repetitive and requires a good deal of patience and coordination. That's why Janet and nearly anybody else operates the transplanter, and I drive the tractor. The tractor driver has to drive straight and slowly—patience and coordination are not part of the job description—just set the throttle and drive straight. To enable machine cultivation, it's important that the rows of transplanted strawberries be a uniform distance from one another, but with a little awareness, a tractor driver can do this. I might add here, though it doesn't pertain to our discussion of transplanting, because the two other persons on the transplanter are located so close to the tractor, it is not an appropriate time for tractor singing unless the singing is done in a very muted voice, at which someone on the transplanter is certain to yell, "What did you say?"

Making things straight in his field is important to a farmer. Regardless of the length of time something may be visible, it's important that it be straight. A windrow of hay may be swallowed by the baler within hours of its creation, but the farmer still feels the need to make it look like a team of surveyors set the course like a taut line from one end of his field to the other. The actor Richard Burton, when he wrote his own eulogy, referenced a Welsh plowman, and it went something like "He kept his own counsel, he worked hard, and could plow a furrow straight." The highest of compliments.

Janet and her brother, Buck, who is six feet four inches tall and weighs north of two hundred fifty pounds, were riding the transplanter, and I was driving the tractor—straight and slow. Go too fast and things happen on the transplanter that the operators can't keep up with. They then become uncoordinated and quickly lose patience and yell at the tractor driver to "Slow down!"

A visit from Buck to the farm was elating for Maggie. He did all the things she liked. He talked to her and scratched her ears, roughed up her thick fur, and pushed her from side to side with just the right amount of rough. Maggie was with us in the strawberry field of course and very interested in Buck. She walked beside Buck on the transplanter, her reward being an occasional word of recognition, or if we were stopped, a loving shove from Buck's meaty hand or scratch behind her ear. I guess she must have gotten bored without Buck's total attention and took to pulling the small transplants out of the ground and returning them to Buck as a token of her caring. I was paying so much attention to Maggie that right after I started yelling, "Maggie, stop pulling the plants out of the ground!" I looked up to see that my heretofore straight row started to look a little like the path the chickens had beaten when eating the tomatoes out of the garden—more than a bit meandering. So much for my semblance to the Welsh plowman.

Maggie then began to walk beside the tractor. She either got disinterested with untransplanting or thought that "Maggie, stop pulling the plants out of the ground!" meant "Come walk very close beside the tractor and distract me from driving straight." If that was her intention, it worked. She walked at the same pace as the tractor and near the front wheel, ever so slightly crowding the tractor's path. As she moved nearer to the wheel, I would minutely steer the tractor away from her and then need to correct my path by first yelling, "Maggie, get out of the way!" and then turning the wheel back to the straight and narrow. Or not so straight and narrow. By the end of the day, we had planted the crookedest field of strawberries in Rockingham County. Maybe New Hampshire. The winding rows meandered more than the subjects of a politician's stump speech.

VERSE 5

I FOUND A HALF-WORN PAIR OF MEN'S SLIPPERS ON OUR LAWN one morning. I knew how they got there. Why they were there would never be answered. I didn't know whose they were. They were better than mine—nice leather and lined with lamb's wool. I placed them on the porch and hoped that the owner, one of our neighbors I was sure, would see them and take them home. By evening, they were gone, but they were back on the lawn a few days later. I placed them on the porch, and again they were gone by evening. Next morning, I looked out to see Maggie, carrying a mouth full of slippers as though delivering the party's nomination to the convention podium, trotting down the road—with a barefoot Jim Falconer, our elderly, retired neighbor to the east, in hot pursuit. By the time Jim, Maggie, and I all met at the edge of my lawn, Jim was puffing and short of breath. I think I saw Maggie smiling. I wasn't smiling. "Doris doesn't want me treading mud in the house, so I keep these slippers in the back hall and take off my boots and put the slippers on when I go inside," Jim said, taking them from the dog's mouth. "Maggie comes in for a treat, and when she leaves, she takes my slippers, and then I find them on your porch!"

"I'm sorry about the slippers, Jim. I hope they're not

damaged. I'll replace them if you think I should," I said. They didn't look like they'd been chewed, just slimed with a bit of dog drool, but I had to ask, "Why do you feed her?"

"She scratches at the back door until we let her in. She's a nice dog, and Doris and I enjoy her company. She curls up on the kitchen floor, and when I sit down in my armchair, she gets up and puts her head in my lap while I scratch her ears," Jim said. "I asked Doris to pick up some of those dog treats at the market. Maggie likes them."

Jim started leaving his slippers on a high shelf, and Maggie stopped stealing them. It brought to mind some of our miscreant candidates and office holders. They let you scratch their *ears, but when they leave, they take more than your slippers. We give them our trust, and then, like Anthony Wiener, they follow their base instincts. Men and women in positions of power seem to jump at any given opportunity to distance themselves from decency and decorum.

VERSE 6

Thatcher used to herd the chickens around—into the road, out of the road, into the barn, out of the barn, into the house … only once.

He was a herding breed of dog, and it was his nature to move things around—never satisfied with the present condition. He had no feelings for the chickens; he neither liked them nor disliked them. He was indifferent to them as fellow members of the farm family, though not indifferent as to their geographic location. Maggie, on the other hand, felt an apparent acrimony toward the chickens. She tolerated them as chicks. She treated the peeping chicks as we did, like a cute curiosity. She'd even lie in the grass and watch them strut around in their way. She'd allow the round little puffballs near, to touch and even peck at her fur, but when they became adults—laying age when they might have done us some economic good—they became the enemy of sorts. The chickens were tolerated but not cared for. They were protected by her but at times needed protection from her.

One night—it was cold but not freezing, so I think it was November—there was a light rain that kept a hush on almost all sound except the struggling cackles from the chicken coop. Chickens are nearly silent creatures until they're disturbed, and then they explode with a swell of atonal noise that's akin to no other. So while nearly everything that isn't beef or fish tastes like chicken, nothing sounds like chicken. The noise had me running from my warm bed in a pair of shorts and—well, that's all—a pair of shorts. I ran from the house, toward the barn, and into the fenced chicken yard just as a big, fifty-pound bull raccoon dragged a flailing chicken through the small door of the coop. In his surprise at seeing me, he dropped the chicken but took only a couple of seconds to decide that I wasn't much of an adversary. I don't know if it was because I didn't look very menacing in shorts or because of the way I was pressing my back against the three-foot-high wire fence of the enclosure. The raccoon moved slowly and deliberately toward me, the chicken forgotten for the moment.

Raccoons are shy, nocturnal animals that have a fondness for my sweet corn and my chickens but are not aggressive unless cornered, protecting their young or sick with rabies. This guy had a clear exit through the gate of the chicken yard, so he wasn't cornered, and I didn't see any young ones. He walked right past the opening to freedom and came growling at me. Rabies is an ancient disease but relatively new to our population of omnivores. The victim becomes infected from the saliva of a rabid animal, usually transferred by a bite that breaks the skin. The disease is fatal for anyone infected—animals and humans alike—unless treatment is started immediately.

I didn't feel good about my situation. The raccoon was moving toward me in a hostile manner, and I didn't have anywhere to run. My immediate plan when he attacked was to use his momentum, lift him up, and throw him over my shoulder and out of the fenced enclosure. My face is no prize, but irrationally, I was most concerned about facial scarring if I wasn't able to lift him cleanly over my head. A coonskin hat is one thing, but a biting, clawing, raccoon pelt ski mask lacked the panache of its more notable headgear cousin, and to try to pass off the ravages on my face as dueling scars would be a mean test of my credibility.

I moved into a corner to limit his approach to directly in front of me, not from the side. I bent my knees, getting ready to execute my admittedly sketchy plan. Cold, thin mud was oozing between my toes, and a drizzly November rain chilled my bare skin. I braced against the fence as the animal came closer. He paused and lowered his rounded body as he coiled his muscular frame to strike. He never had a chance. Maggie leapt over the fence beside me as easily as if it was plow furrow. She lifted the growling raccoon in her jaws and shook him like he was made of no more than corn husks, instantly snapping his spine with an attack that started and ended before I could take a breath. Neither animal made a sound; the raccoon's life left him before he could voice a protest, and all of Maggie's effort went into killing, with nothing left for expression. I was dumbstruck.

She gave the raccoon a few added shakes, but I could tell by her almost casual effort that she knew they were unnecessary—just a victory celebration, like a running back who throws his arms up after a touchdown. She left the raccoon lying in the mud and went to sniff the chicken that was going to be the wild animal's meal. The bird was injured and bleeding badly near the coop door. Maggie dispatched the chicken with a fraction of the effort needed for the raccoon, then turned and trotted out of the pen and toward the house, leaving the three of us, alive and dead, soaking in the drizzling rain.

She reappeared a few minutes later as I finished cleaning up her handiwork and stood by me, looking for some attention. I bent and gave her thick neck a good hug, exposing myself to the slick of raccoon saliva glistening on her fur.

"I don't approve of (this) conflict," our candidates tell us, "but there are occasions when war is unavoidable." I never heard a candidate speak in favor of conflict; that wouldn't be befitting of our genteel society. And our candidate turned world leader would then have to admit that he also accepted telling mothers and fathers that their sons and daughters were dying for something that our candidate promoted. He'd have to assume that everyone else believed in it. Maggie must have thought of the chickens the way congressmen think about us. I don't mean to say that congressmen want to kill us the way Maggie did chickens, but she only tolerated the chickens. They were, in a sense, part of her farm responsibilities.

The following morning, I called the State Fish and Game Department to ask about rabid raccoons, and according to my description of events, I was told it was reasonable that the animal was rabid. A game warden came by and picked up the carcass around noon the same day to test for disease and told me that even though our dogs were inoculated against rabies, Maggie should get a rabies booster from the vet. This wouldn't be Maggie's last rabies booster. He also suggested that if I was so inclined as to hug my dog, I should call my physician.

"She killed this raccoon?" the warden asked, looking Maggie over for bites or cuts while she tried to lick his face. "Most dogs get beat up pretty bad by a coon this size. It's unusual that she hasn't a bite."

"She did it in less than a heartbeat," I answered. While I showed him the scene of the crime, giving him the full dramatic narrative, although I don't think I mentioned that I was dressed only in shorts, Maggie jumped through his truck window, cutting deep gouges in the paint on the door with her scrambling back claws, and ate whatever remained of his lunch.

VERSE 7

THE EPISODES ON ROUTE 150 STARTED GETTING OUT OF HAND again. Chief Aquilina brought Maggie home in the squad car one evening with a stern warning that her behavior couldn't continue. "The dog will have to be restrained, or I'll have to re-strain her myself," he said, brushing the mud from her grimy feet off the seat of the cruiser. "The dog" was excited to ride with the chief. She sat erect in the seat beside him, drooling lightly on his uniformed shoulder. She looked as a Dalmatian might appear in a fire truck—maybe a little less regal and a little more rural.

I don't remember if that's when I told him, "I live on a one-hundred-fifty-acre farm and shouldn't have to tie up my dog!" or if it was another time when he told me I had to re-strain the dog. I do recall his polite response, or at least words to the effect "If she stayed on your one-hundred-fifty-acre farm, there wouldn't be this problem."

Things really came to a head one Saturday morning in June. I remember that it was June because it was strawberry season. We had a couple of acres of pick-your-own berries, and we were busy with customers, showing them where to go in the field to pick, weighing their pickings, and making change. Maggie had been with us for a couple of years by then, and we had lost track of her goings. I should say comings and goings, but there were many more goings than comings. The police cruiser drove slowly by our farm and parked on the edge of the road because our customers' cars had filled our driveway. I was hoping the visit by the chief was because of our overcrowded parking issue and not the *other* issue. My hopes were groundless. "Dave, I've taken Maggie to the pound. I found her on Route 150 last night, and you're aware of my previous warnings. You haven't paid your dog tax this year either. If you pay the dog tax on Monday when the town office opens, you can get her out. Because I had to pick her up, it's going to be twenty-five dollars for her release."

We considered this a sign. The pound was operated by our local veterinarian, Bob Marston. Bob had his practice in Amesbury but operated a small farm in East Kingston, our neighboring town. Stray dogs and other animals were impounded on his farm and then released to the owners or taken to the SPCA shelter in Stratham. Because he was a veterinarian, he could also deal with animals' health issues or put them down if that were the case.

The heat of the day drives strawberry pickers out of the field and into their cool homes, so it was late morning before our last customer had gone and Janet and I could sit down for a serious discussion. We knew that we had failed to keep the dog on the farm, and maybe it was time to bring the Maggie era to a close. Bob Marston had the dog and the means to put an end to her constant roaming. She was, sooner or later, going to be hit and killed or injured by a car either on Route 150 or crossing some other road between our farm and, who knew, maybe the Massachusetts border. We loved the dog and were charmed by her antics and exuberance, but we knew that we would eventually be stricken by a sad ending—an ending that would not only bring her injury and unnecessary pain but could cause an accident that might be harmful to an innocent driver or passenger. The sad ending would come about by a simple phone call.

After a lot of discussion, I made the call. I said to Debbie Marston, Bob's wife, after she confirmed that Maggie was in a pen in their barn, "We've tried everything we know to keep the dog close to the farm, but we haven't been successful. We don't want to give up on her, and I don't want to chain her to a doghouse, but we've reached the end of our patience. Before the dog does serious harm to herself or someone else, we'd like to have Bob put her down."

Debbie said she understood how we felt and she'd ask her husband to do it for us. He'd call afterward, and we could pick her up and bury her remains. It wouldn't happen that day because he was busy but probably by the first of the week. If we changed our mind, call, but otherwise …

A dark cloud descended over us for the rest of the day. I felt like a coward for asking someone else to fix our problem, a failure for not being able to keep the dog out of trouble, and a Judas for turning my back on a good friend. I know, it's a dog we're talking about here, but she had, some time ago, taken that leap in our consciousness from being a pet to a valued member of our family. Janet and I cried, reasoned, and tried to vindicate ourselves and overcome our sadness. After a sleepless night and a long, pensive day, we had come to grips with what we had done, and by the end of Monday, we were, if not satisfied, at least accepting of our decision. Bob hadn't called us to pick up the body but would the next day, and we could put to rest the Maggie phenomenon.

It rained hard on Monday night. The strawberry beds were muddy and had to dry out for a few hours before our customers could pick. There were large puddles in our yard and in the ever-present potholes on Moulton Ridge Road. One customer had arrived, and he and I were talking, standing beside his car, when my attention was drawn to the road. There, running with abandon through the steam rising from the warming pavement, jumping like a slalom skier from puddle to puddle, and splashing water all over the road with her huge feet was Maggie! She made straight for us. I knew she'd jump on our customer with those enormous, wet, muddy feet.

I knew this dog would do the wrong thing and … she didn't!

She did jump up on me with those enormous, wet, muddy feet, but I'd come to expect nothing less.

If our corn had popped on the cob, I couldn't have been more surprised! Shocked was a better word. Everything I felt about Maggie had come and gone. Janet and I had dealt with her passing as though she was already in the ground. In our minds and hearts, she was no longer with us, and yet here she was, soaking wet, mud up to her belly, her wet coat smelling of swamp and decaying vegetation, lively as the last time I saw her, leaning against me, pushing on me with her tremendous weight and strength, every bit as alive as she was on Friday when she had been with us last.

Janet came ashen faced from the back door, wrapped her arms around the dog's dripping neck, and through joyful tears said, "I just got off the phone with Bob Marston. Somehow Maggie escaped the pen he kept her in, got out of his barn, went through an electric sheep fence, and scaled a six-foot chain-link fence that surrounds his farm. He said we should expect her here any minute! I see that Bob's estimate was off by at least one minute.

"I saw you and Maggie through the window just before Bob called, and I thought that you'd changed your mind and called Bob to get her back," Janet said.

"Nothing could be further from the truth. I thought the deal was done—that we were finished with our little problem here. I didn't expect this," I said, scratching Maggie's ears.

"Bob said to bring her back if we wanted," Janet said, avoiding the words "if we still want her put down."

We looked at each other and the dog, and without further comment, I said, "No. I'll just go to the town office and pay the dog tax. I'll get Thatcher licensed at the same time."

With two legally licensed dogs, we settled back for a normal summer on the farm. To our surprise, Maggie stopped traveling like she needed a passport. She stayed pretty close to the farm. Oh, I still saw her a lot at Jim and Doris's or looking at me through Rudy's screen door as I passed by, but I didn't see Chief Aquilina all summer. She rid us of at least a dozen woodchucks that season. I know there were no less than a dozen because that's the number of carcasses I found on the lawn and needed to bury.

VERSE 8

Janet and I usually walk in the mornings. It's about a mile from our farm past the pond and Rudy's house, across Hilliard Road and on to the top of Moulton Ridge. At six in the morning, there's little traffic, so we try to walk every day at that time, usually with Maggie, Thatcher, and Pete, our black-and-white cat.

Kensington has rubbish collection early on Tuesday mornings, so everyone puts their bags and barrels of trash out by the road on Monday night. One clear Tuesday morning in July, as we neared Rudy's house, we saw a trash bag ripped apart and its contents strewn all over his lawn. His lawn is the pride of the neighborhood. It's as well groomed as a candidate greeting parishioners at church. Rudy has his lawn tended by Cheeza's Lawn Service. Weekly, professional landscapers trim his lawn with commercial mowers and engine-powered trimmers and mulchers. Rudy's lawn is pristine. Our lawn, on the other hand, has the appearance of being mowed by sheep, but if I have the bush hog attached to the tractor, I'll run over it to even it out some. I'm not sure that Janet likes my lawn-maintenance program, but like most farmers, we make do.

Anyway, this wasn't a plastic bag that ripped open, leaving

its contents in a brief pile a few feet square near the bag. Oh no! Rudy's lawn looked like the first snow had happened in July! His lawn was white with napkins, pizza boxes, paper towels—all the things a normal family uses and disposes of in a normal week. It had to be Maggie's doing. There was no other explanation. She must have come up during the night or an hour before we walked and, while examining Rudy's trash for contraband (anything edible or close to edible), made this mess. We panicked! Rudy was as considerate as a neighbor could be, but his good nature would be tested when he saw his weekly collection strewn across his evenly clipped, dark green lawn. "We've got to clean it up before Rudy sees it!" Janet said.

I was a little more optimistic. "Maybe the wind will blow it away," I said.

"Don't be ridiculous!" Janet said, with that incredulous look that she reserved for a candidate who claimed he'd lower our taxes. "Besides, it will all blow to our house."

To me, she said, "Help me clean it up." Maggie understood Janet to say, "Let's scatter Rudy's trash over the largest area possible. Gambol over his lawn and even bark a little. He might come out and join us. This will really be fun!" As the humans started collecting, Maggie started spreading. Strewing is closer akin to her actions because spreading suggests some organization. She was joyous! She shredded a pizza box and scattered the remains into the air like confetti at a political convention. She ripped an Exeter News Letter that must have lined Rudy's bird cage out of my hands and teased me with it until I chased her all the way to Rudy's garage. I remember seeing the smeared image of our next president on the front page just before Maggie ripped him out of my hands and ran.

Janet was starting a pile of Rudy's refuse near the road. I didn't know what Janet was going to do with the pile, but Maggie knew what *she* was going to do with it. My kids used to do the same thing with piles of autumn leaves. Jump into the pile like a tornado and make it explode. Thatcher and the cat watched us quietly from the road, probably keeping score of this little exercise: "Maggie six, incompetent humans nothing."

Maggie made a paper-plate flowerbed, a tattered-egg-carton hedge, and a few sketchily designed plantings of bread wrappers. She did some thoughtful scatterings with yellow napkins to resemble dandelions blossoming in the lush grass. I thought that might upset Rudy as much as anything. With the delicate touch of a bulldozer, she lined the driveway with a discarded paper milk carton. For an instant, I wished Maggie's face was on the milk carton. "Missing dog. Hope she stays that way. Don't trouble yourself to find her."

Maggie was draping the forsythia that grew along the front of the house with facial tissues when Rudy stepped from his front door. Maggie ran up the three steps and greeted him and then turned to sit beside him and watch Janet and me as we continued collecting our neighbor's litter. After a silent moment, Rudy and Maggie turned and entered the house, Rudy probably back to bed and Maggie to watch Janet and me through his screen door. As we finished collecting, Rudy reappeared at the door and opened it. He held out a substitute plastic trash bag to Maggie who, bounding and joyous, delivered it to us as per Rudy's unspoken directions. I think Rudy was smiling. I know Maggie was.

VERSE 9

PRECIPITOUS IS NOT A FARM KIND OF WORD. WE DON'T USE the word *precipitous* often, if at all. *Plunging* might be used with regard to a toilet plunger, or *steep* to describe the rise in fuel prices, but the only derivative of precipitous for farm use would be precipitation, which of course carries great interest. A presidential candidate might have more use for the word precipitous, as in a precipitous drop in his poll numbers following a particularly glaring misstep at a press conference or a precipitous rise in his/her campaign debt. Candidates have greater concern with the elements of precipitousness than farmers. Things generally go pretty slow on a farm; abrupt changes seldom happen. Events this year are little changed from events of last year, except that fertilizer costs more, but that's as predictable as precipitation in April.

Our candidates are always trying to change events. It's in their best interest to have events change precipitously and, in so doing, generate news interest. A headline "Nothing Happened Today on the Campaign Trail" is not a headline at all. It's not even a footnote. "The Candidate Has Made a Precipitous Change Today" is a real headline. It generates interest.

I'm going on about *precipitous* because it's the only way I can describe the drop in our egg production. To say *steep* would do the trick, but it doesn't adequately describe the precipitousness of the fall. We're not in the egg business. Our income doesn't depend on our egg production. We have only a handful of chickens, and they produce enough eggs for our family, and if we have a few dozen extra, Janet will put them on a card table near the road, and the neighbors enjoy fresh eggs for less than the grocery store sells them.

I placed a Have-A-Heart trap near the chicken coop, hoping that I might catch a raccoon, although I thought a raccoon would probably eat more than just the eggs. He'd probably take an egg layer or two or more, and we hadn't been losing any chickens.

Our very joyous friend Howdy Morgan stopped at the farm one autumn afternoon. One of our many interesting friends, Howdy was a teacher, before that a brick mason, before that a pig farmer, and previous to that, while at MIT, he designed the guidance system for the space shuttle. Yes, NASA's own space shuttle. We never really knew a reason for this progression, but we appreciated that Howdy lived near us and not in some physics laboratory in Cambridge.

I describe Howdy as joyous because that's the only way to portray him. He was so awesomely intelligent he understood and pierced through to the essence of everything, winnowed away the gravity like a lifeless husk, and harvested the shining kernel of humor. Everything was a joke to Howdy. If taxes went up (yeah, *if* taxes went up; *when* taxes went up), he'd find some absurdity in *why* taxes went up. There was always plenty of fuel for his humor in our perennial presidential primary. A candidate only had to show up, and Howdy would have us entertained by either a misstep or no misstep. I'm sorry that he missed the forty-fifth president; he'd have reaped four years of enjoyment. His laugh rolled up from his core; like thunder approaching from the western hills, it started low and so deep as to hardly be heard and built up to a wonderfully engaging roar as insistent as a campaign ad.

Everything about Howdy was oversized—his intellect, his enthusiasm, his body, his laugh, and his absurdity. No joke could be told without a billowing, belly-shaking laugh. No narrative could be passed along without an unsuppressed giggle. Elected officials were his primary target, persons appointed to office were next, and maybe last, though not least by any means, was anyone forward enough to write a letter to an editor. Howdy had two vehicles, a well-used dump truck and an old VW—both short a few bolts that kept the frame and chassis a bonded unit, and from the barn where I was shelling popcorn, it was the VW that I heard rattle into our yard. Nothing seemed unusual. The car fenders sang a metallic chorus, the partially dislocated door creaked open and slammed shut, and the driver laughed loudly. All as it should be, but the joy became a little too joyous; the delight too delightful; his laugh, always infectious, was bordering on hysteria. I peered through one of the cracked, cobweb-obscured windows in the barn and saw Howdy leaning red-faced against his car, laughing uncontrollably at something in the direction of the chicken coop. Janet, drawn by Howdy's amusement, had come from the house and for a moment was as transfixed as I was but was soon laughing too.

When Howdy saw me come from the barn, he choked out, "That's the biggest yellow chicken I've ever seen! Not that I've ever seen a yellow chicken like that!"

Maggie was several sizes larger than the door that the chickens used to get into their coop, but that hadn't stopped her from squeezing in, and now all that appeared through the opening was her massive head, looking out like something mounted by a mad taxidermist. Janet opened the people door, and Maggie bounded out, feathers and dust flying as she ran straight to greet Howdy.

Something wasn't right. She didn't look at either Janet or me, and her face looked somehow full. Her cheeks, if a dog has cheeks, were distended and puffy. Her jaws were slightly apart, and her gaze, even though she was trotting toward Howdy, was focused in a direction away from all of us. I called her, and she ignored me. Howdy called her, and she glanced at him but turned away and trotted toward the field of corn.

Janet called her name firmly, like she would an errant child, and the dog stopped but wouldn't turn around. She kept facing the cornfield. The three of us approached her, and Maggie took a hesitant step away and toward the corn.

"Maggie, stop!" Janet called again, and the big animal stopped again but still didn't turn in our direction.

After several more tentative steps, we caught up with her, but when I placed my hand between her ears, she turned her head away from me. She jerked back when I placed my hand on her muzzle and shook her head slightly when I raised one of her lips. She didn't want me looking in her mouth. Howdy still thought this the funniest thing he'd seen all day, or all week for that matter, and as his laughter infected Janet, Maggie thought this a good opportunity to join in the fun and started prancing away from me. She slipped my grip on her muzzle, and I reached out for any dog part I could find as she danced away. The best I could do was her long tail, and so we began a comic parade, dog and man, along the dirt drive and once again in the direction of the cornfield. Happy days are here again!

The epic battle of good versus evil raged on through the lower yard and on toward the cornfield. I was the good element, for I had ownership on my side. Whatever was in her mouth that came out of the chicken coop was mine because I had purchased the chickens. Okay, some of our chickens were a birthday gift to Janet from her friend Pat, and another bunch were the end result of a fourth-grade science experiment in hatching eggs, but I paid for the grain the chickens ate. Besides, I am human, and I have intellect. Alright, I was hanging on to a dog's tail and probably didn't look very intellectual, but still, my human intelligence should count for something.

Janet and Howdy were no help. The farther Maggie pulled me toward the corn, the harder those two laughed and the more Maggie was convinced that this was a romping good game. I could have just let go and our little procession would have ended, but I was determined by now to see what was in her mouth, and I knew that if I didn't stop her here and now, I would always suspect but never know for sure.

Like a congressional truth commission (now there's an oxymoron), if you're persistent and ask enough questions, you'll learn the truth. If I hung on to that thick yellow and white tail long enough, I too might learn the truth. All the jostling and running, all of Maggie's intensity to get away from me caused her to clamp her jaws closed just a little but enough to crack one of those delicate delicacies she had in her mouth. Egg white and yolk seeped down her jowls. She stopped because she couldn't bear the loss of a midday snack, so she bowed her head and opened her mouth to release at least three whole eggs and two that had cracked during our little dance. She started to lick up the contents of the broken ones.

I reached to pick up the dog-drool-covered but otherwise undamaged remains, only to get into a snatching contest with the dog who was not content to leave the whole eggs for me. Maggie had a good-natured wag going with her tail and a thumping, prancing crouch with her front legs, but I wasn't nearly as happy. I had two of the eggs in my hand, but she grabbed the remaining three before I could react and was again headed for the cornfield with them.

"Leave her alone, Dave" was Janet's advice when I started after the dog. "She won!"

She did win! Until then, I hadn't known that life with a dog was a contest. Now I realized that living around Maggie was a campaign with winners and losers. And there was a clear distinction between them—no gray area.

"Well, Howdy," I said. "It's good to see you. Anything special today or just a neighborly visit? I'm glad that we had the opportunity to entertain you." I must have emitted a little sarcasm because Janet looked at me like a candidate would look at a vice president with a good idea.

Barely able to speak through his laughter, he managed to say, "Thought I'd see if you had any eggs!"

I wonder what life is like for a presidential candidate the day following a lost election. Primary elections differ from a regular election because all candidates in the field count their votes. Figuratively they count their votes. Election workers actually do the counting; candidates do the worrying. In a regular election, the candidate with the most votes wins. In a primary election, a candidate with fewer votes than the winner can still be a winner if he/she gets more votes than expected. In this way, a winner (the candidate with the most votes but fewer votes than expected) can be a loser, and a loser (a candidate with fewer votes but more votes than expected) can be a winner. The faction that controls the outcome of an election in this case is the pollster who does nothing but sit in an office (probably without windows), call people on the phone, and ask them who they prefer as their next presidential candidate. The less accurate their prediction, the greater the opportunity for an upset.

I suspect that the day an election is lost must be quite different from any other day. Campaign staff, supporters, and the press are as eager as always to commiserate, compare notes, and wind down the frantic machine that was an election campaign, but the following morning must be like waking up in a desert.

VERSE 10

Our presidential candidates seem to arrive in our fair state every year. They don't show up just in an election year; they start testing the waters (polluting the waters might be more accurate) the day after the presidential election. Because of this prolonged election process, we New Hampshireites (that's probably not the right term, but citizens of New Hampshire anyway) may have a more cynical view of the election process than the rest of the country. It's not that we don't appreciate the democratic right to vote. It isn't that at all. In fact, I think that we have a greater appreciation of that right, reinforced by our nearly perpetual exposure to the process and the personalities. We're schooled from an early age to recognize, understand, and participate in the great quad-annual (every four years?) election event that happens in the United States, but even hay weather—warm, sunny days made for drying hay—requires a break once in a while.

My point is not so much a discussion on the democratic tradition, rather to compare the arrival of our candidates, which happens every year, and the arrival of the flu. I came down with a good case of the flu one winter, and it lasted for a little more than the standard twenty-four hours. I was going on the third day and was becoming stir-crazy in bed and so decided to move to the living room couch. Maggie enjoyed a good, stout piece of furniture just as much as the rest of us. We discouraged her from getting on the furniture, but Maggie was a tough one to discourage. I was stretched out under several blankets, and the TV was on—tuned in to something but I don't remember what, probably a candidate's press conference, an event easy to forget—when Maggie came and sat on the floor beside me. She leaned her head against me, so I idly scratched her ears. She'd been out in the snow, and her fur was damp and cold, and she smelled a little like mittens drying on a radiator.

Where I scratched under her ears, it was warm; her whole body felt warm as I pushed my fingers under her coat. The more I pet her, the more she leaned against me, and finally she became so relaxed that her large feet lost traction and she slid to the floor out of my scratching reach. She was quickly up and placed one wet paw on top of my stacked blankets, so I resumed my ear scratching. After several minutes, she relaxed and found herself on the floor again. This time, I reached down and scratched her ears while she was lying down, but that wasn't her plan.

She stood beside me again but this time raised herself on her back legs and placed both front legs and half of her sizable weight on top of my chest. I pushed her off, and she repeated the move two more times until I gave up on pushing her off and stroked beneath her ears again. After a minute or two of that, she managed to awkwardly place two front feet on my chest, and one back foot on the couch beside me, which left one foot on the floor and three feet on either me or the couch.

This arrangement remained for about two minutes, and then partly by leaning and partly by pushing with her legs, she rolled her entire self on top of me. I was like chrysalis in the blankets, unable to move, and she jostled and adjusted her position, digging into me with dog elbows and knees until she was lying flat on top of me, her two huge front paws just under my chin and the rest of her solid body stretched out over mine. She exhaled a colossal sigh of dog breath in my face and settled herself in for, I'm sure she thought, the evening. I tried to roll her off, but my arms were pinioned under the blankets. I couldn't sit up with a hundred-odd-pound parcel of dog on top of me, so I did the only thing I could do. I called Janet.

After the last three days of my calling Janet—I was sick, you understand—she was a little less responsive on day three than she had been on day one. Three times less responsive, and from my perspective, maybe even more than that. By the time she arrived, I was having a little difficulty filling my lungs due to the oppressive weight on my diaphragm. A torture like this was probably quite popular during the Spanish Inquisition, or maybe the CIA used something like this and called it *dog boarding*. Anyway, Janet finally did arrive and knew exactly what to do. "Oh! Stay right there. I'll go get the camera," she said excitedly. Like I was going anywhere soon. "The kids are going to love this!" I would have preferred a cattle prod to a camera.

The picture is still in our Maggie collection. The dog inclined her head toward the camera, just enough to avoid red eye, I'm sure, and she looks very comfortable, maybe even a little smug. I look like I felt, like I was being crushed, because I was being crushed. I now know how an apple feels in a cider press. I have new sympathy for them, though I still enjoy cider and cider doughnuts even more.

Sounding like the last breath of a deflating air mattress, I managed to croak, "Get the dog off me." I even managed a "Please!" But when Janet called Maggie, the mountain of rank-smelling fur did a small shift of her body to the inside of the couch, not toward the floor on the outside. All this time, the dog gazed languidly at a spot somewhere over my head and in back of me, like I wasn't even there. She probably thought of me as an inconvenient lump in her otherwise soft and comfortable bed.

Her nose was not more than an inch or two from mine, with her hot breath softly blowing into my face. I started to ask myself what the last thing was that Maggie might have eaten. Knowing her, it could have been anything. Once, I took away the black, swollen carcass of a long-dead beaver that she had carried onto our lawn and was getting ready to roll onto. I couldn't imagine where she had found it, but as she was lying there on top of me, hot wisps of her breath wafting onto my face, I remembered her with that beaver, and the same thought that I had that day on the lawn came back to me. *Ugh, she picked that thing up in her mouth. What could it possibly have tasted like?* And now that same mouth was nearly touching me.

I struggled a little more to get free, but her four legs slid down the sides of my body and tightened the blankets around my arms, entrapping me even more. Also, with each little shift of my body, she made a slight movement toward the inside of the couch, moving me more to the outside. She started doing a contented little pant. This accomplished two things: one, it increased the volume of dog breath blowing on me; and two, it gave her body a slight but rapid up-and-down rhythm that, like an iron lung run amok, threatened to crush my stomach and chest with each downward compression.

"How are you feeling, Dave?" Janet wanted to know. She had taken her picture and was returning to whatever she was doing in another room.

I couldn't gain enough breath in my lungs to answer, but the unspoken reply was, "How do you think I feel? I've had the flu for three days, and now this oversized excuse for a family pet is slowly crushing me, and you ask how do I feel?"

"I'll be in the kitchen. Call if you need anything."

None of the occupants of the couch so much as murmured, for differing reasons of course. One hadn't the physical capacity to murmur, and the other couldn't have been more content. I supposed if Maggie had considered, she might have asked for a snack—any leftover beef in the refrigerator for instance.

As I heard Janet's footsteps fading down the hall and away from any help she might have given me, I realized that I was truly on my own. Pete, the cat, walked through the living room and hardly glanced at the dog and me on the couch. Whatever the struggle or situation going on there was beneath his concern. He walked through the room and then returned to jump onto the stuffed chair across from the couch, laid his head on his paws, and, with tiny slits for eyes, watched the entertainment.

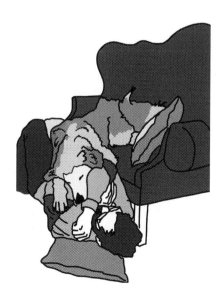

By now, Maggie had shifted 10 percent of her weight to the inside of the couch. This had two effects: it allowed me to breathe a little more easily but also began an unhurried but eventual displacement of my body with hers. Her bearing didn't change. She still continued to gaze at the wallpaper and pant contentedly.

The outcome was as certain as corn borer as she moved predictably into that space between me and the back of the couch. It took her twenty minutes or so to do it, but soon I was on the floor, without the blankets, and she, with a deep sigh, closed her eyes and fell asleep on top of the two blankets and on top of the couch. I lay there for a moment or two, considering how I might get back under my blankets and onto the couch, but gave it up as a lost cause. I crossed the room with the thought of displacing the cat on the wingback chair, but like one of the losers on primary day, I decided to go upstairs and consider my next strategy, in my bed. I'd be comfortable there until Maggie decided that the couch might be a little firm or the blankets lumpy.

VERSE 11

Maggie was my dog. She was brought to the farm by Janet with the support of her friend Pat and our daughter Kelly but when in the house, Maggie sat or lay near me, and when I went to the barn or fields, we went together. While I shelled beans or transplanted seedlings or stacked bales of straw in the barn, she would lay near my feet or comfort herself in the straw. She was more at home in the barn than in the house. She could chase mice with the cats, snuffle around the centuries-old building, revisiting ancient smells of cows, horses, and other livestock, and though she liked the living room couch, for Maggie, there was nothing quite as accommodating as a bed of straw to stretch in and ponder the day's events.

In the fields, she was with me whether I was on a tractor or afoot, picking corn or cutting firewood on the fence line. She traveled to all corners of the field or woodlot, her nose either raised in a salute to scents carried on the breeze or snuffling the ground like a canine Sherlock Holmes, her lofty tail always curled upward like a large, feathery sickle. If I stayed for an hour or for the day, she remained with me, not always within sight, but we always sensed each other. Like a candidate in the closing days before the primary, she was never far away.

She crashed through the woodlots like a gold and white

bulldozer. She would go over or through a thicket of brush before she would go around it—partly because the shortest distance between two points is a straight line but also because she might stir up a rabbit or chipmunk, and there is nothing quite as much fun as a good race with a cottontail or to try to follow a squirrel up a tree. Her fur was a constant tangle of briers and burdocks, and we spent many a quiet evening with a dog brush cleaning out her coat. We called her "the dirty old, smelly old dog." Thatcher was the exact opposite. He would walk around the rain puddle that Maggie would walk through. When the fields were muddy in the spring, Thatcher would skirt the edges, while Maggie would romp festively through the wettest, muddiest section of field she could find. Where she slept overnight, there would be a moderate pile of sandy loam in the morning, released like granular prisoners as they fell from her drying coat.

Maggie never saw a patch of earth that couldn't be improved with a hole, which she would create, usually to the depth of a Malaysian tiger trap. A relentless digger, she felt that the earth beneath her feet always needed to be transformed. I had an aunt who felt that way about her furniture; it was always in the wrong place and had to be relocated. Some of Maggie's excavations still remain like open mine pits that have yet to be reclaimed. There's one about a foot deep next to the old carriage shed beside the house. It's near the path I follow when I bring in firewood, and sometimes I fall into it when it's covered with snow. I curse, struggle to right myself, and swear that I'll fill it in when the ground thaws in the spring, but it remains today, a relic of her existence and confirmation of my reluctance to close her out of our lives.

One of her favorite operations of soil relocation took place in the fall when I harvested potatoes. Potatoes are a tuber that grows beneath the soil's surface and are harvested with a garden fork. She applied herself to digging potatoes with the vigor of a handshaking presidential candidate. Her powerful body and shovel-sized feet were the perfect adaptation for throwing dirt. Even our New Hampshire fieldstones didn't slow her much. When she bent to her task, using both an alternating paw and a double-pawed technique, great plumes of soil, rocks, and potatoes flew across the garden like ICBMs. My job would have been easier had I not needed to walk a twenty-foot circle with my basket and retrieve the spent missiles, but it was probably less work than if I had to dig them up myself. Everything flew in a grand arc between her back legs in a spray of debris. Her method was surprisingly gentle to the potatoes; they didn't receive so much as a scratch from her hardened claws, and the resultant holes in the garden would fill in when I plowed in the spring.

Maggie loved snow. The first flakes in November brought out the puppy in her. When she was excited, she did a bouncing dance. She would spin in a circle, her front feet hopping in a larger arc than her back feet. The number of rotations she made indicated how excited she was. One rotation for minor excitement, like a treat tossed to her by the letter carrier. Two spins for a family member who came home after being gone for the day. Three spins for a visit from Howdy, Charlie, or Buck. Snow, however, especially those first few flakes that declare the coming of winter, would bring on spins without number. She would leap joyously out of the house and into the yard and become the whirling dervish of dogs, spinning repeatedly in happy circles that carried her across the lawn and crashing into the tall, frozen remnants of sunflower stalks. I believe her act of whirling dervishly was her tribute to a higher power, except that she whirled with greater devotion, commitment, and joy than the original Eastern whirlers, though she might lack their grace and stature.

To be caught in her revolving arc was equivalent to being hit by a truck. When the mass of a spiraling, hundred-pound-plus dog collides with a relatively unstable and movable two-legged object, there can only be one result, and it ain't good—or comforting. I was on the receiving end enough times to know to head for higher ground when the spin got underway. Maggie thought a good, sturdy collision was part of the routine, and it usually encouraged her into a more furious whirl. She was so excited by a gathering of red-coated, mounted fox hunters and their stately horses milling around our door yard one crisp September Saturday that her spin and collision put a good dent in the front fender of the pickup. It stood as a warning to anyone who took her antics lightly. If an innocent person didn't feel the need to put a little distance between themselves and the whirler, we'd show them the dent and say something to the effect of "This is your body, and this is your body after Maggie has run over you." The dent remains, though the truck was retired two years ago and we pushed it into the woods with the other farm relics.

Her coat was thick and dense as a sheep, the perfect wrap for New Hampshire in January. Give her a trunk for a nose and smutty up the yellow color, and there you'd have a wooly mammoth. All winter, she would recline in the yard like a sovereign on her bed of ice and snow. I saw her completely covered by a one-foot snowstorm, only to remove herself to the house like the abominable snow dog, leaving melting puddles in her wake because she was reluctant to shake off the snow that was keeping her cool. As spring approached, she'd seek out like a hunter the diminishing orphaned snowbanks that hid in the shade, loath to leave us for the season. She'd cling to them as though to prevent them melting away before the snows of the next winter. In summer, she escaped the daytime heat by standing up to her neck in the pond, always followed by a good roll on the muddy bank, proceeded by a leisurely walk to the house and, if no one was around to stop her, a nice nap on the couch. All evenings, summer or winter, were spent like a traveler, off to the next town, a brisk walk to the town park to take in a Little League game, or maybe just to Route 150 to see what Chief Aquilina was up to.

If you asked Janet, she would say that Maggie was her dog. When I returned from whatever Maggie and I had been doing, Janet would tell me with conviction that Maggie had been with her all the time she was picking blueberries, canning peaches, preparing a lesson plan for a student, or whatever. Rudy Hede and Jim Falconer probably also believed that Maggie was their dog, and I still hold to the belief that somewhere within a twenty-mile radius of our farm, there exists some household who also believed that Maggie was their family pet. She was, in a sense, a sort of polygamist. Our successful candidates have a quality that assures you that they are concerned only with your interests. They'd have you believe that they've been with you all day; and with your neighbor all day; and with your spouse. They speak in a tongue understood by all and by no one. It's possible to fool all the people …

VERSE 12

IT HAD RAINED DURING THE NIGHT, AND THE AIR HUNG heavy with a misty fog that still hadn't burned off as we walked through our woodlot. I had worn the wrong shoes for walking that morning, and my sodden Nikes squished on my feet. Janet wore leather hiking boots—waterproof leather hiking boots—and Maggie, of course, wore no shoes at all. For a while, the sucking sound generated by my feet was the only sound we heard, until it was overwhelmed by a troop of hiking Boy Scouts, a contingent of a weekend jamboree held at the town park. Excitement like cool water from a spring bubbled from the collection of boys sharing the possibilities of what might be hiding around the next corner or group of trees. Any game or wild animals, of course, were sent running by the alarm set off by the cannonade of preadolescent voices, but a big yellow dog responds more like water to dry Nikes than water off a duck. Janet and I stepped to the edge of the path while the troop jostled past us, but Maggie strutted into the middle of the pack, looking up with a panting joy into each happy face, and was swept away into the tide of laughing hikers. We continued home, sans dog, my wet sponge feet squishing with each step, Janet occasionally suggesting that shoes of a more waterproof construction might have been a better wardrobe choice. I noted her leather boots, but I had no comment.

When Maggie didn't return by late afternoon, I drove the pickup to the town park, assuming she would be there working on her merit badge for chasing frogs or stealing food from young campers. The park was a hive of Scouts laughing and running through a thicket of pup tents and smoking campfires laid out over the ball field, producing a sound level equal to a squadron of F-18s taking off from Pease Air Base.

I chartered a course to the biggest tent, where I found an adult stretched out as best as he could in a folding camp chair, eyes closed, a copy of The Boy Scout Manual opened on his lap, and successfully keeping out the noise of the crowd with a large pair of stereo headphones fitted snugly over his ears. The plug end of the headphones lay unplugged into anything on the grass beneath his camp chair. "I think she's with Troop A from Kingston," the Scout leader yawned as he told me. "They were cooking hot dogs over a campfire in right field, and she was pretty involved."

I went to right field and Troop A from Kingston, only to be told that the hot dog roast was over, that the live dog had an ample number of hot dogs, and I was redirected to Troop A or C from Exeter—left field. The Exeter group told me that she was there for a tug-of-war but left with a troop from Brentwood who were having knot-tying instruction—in home run territory. It was then that I saw her racing off into the woods with a group of boys and adults armed with bow saws and hatchets to retrieve firewood. I was starting to feel like a presidential candidate trying to catch up with the press corps. It's tough to be effective if no one knows you're there.

I was sure of three things. One, to call her with the volume necessary for her to hear me at that distance and over the din of exited Boy Scouts would be beyond my vocal range—even though my voice was well tuned from tractor singing. Two, it might be a little strange for one of the few adults present to be yelling, "Margaret," at the top of his voice. And three, if I were capable of calling loud enough for her to hear me, and if it didn't seem a little bizarre, yelling a female name while standing amid a collection of boys, Maggie would just ignore me and continue on her way, a strategic member of the wood-cutting detail.

One of the things that the owners of errant dogs and failing presidential candidates must learn is when to quit the field. All I needed to do was drive off in my pickup. A candidate does practically the same thing, but he must recognize the efforts of his campaign staff, thank all those who supported him, and, most difficult of all, say something nice about those who defeated him. That's a little tougher. You've spent the last several months—maybe years—lobbing verbal grenades at each other, stopping just short of noting his mother's footwear, and now you must encourage him and his supporters to carry on the good fight. Ugh! Only a politician could conduct himself so. Farmers and chiefs of police could never act on that level. After all, farmers and chiefs of police have their … pride?

If I were a candidate who'd just figured out that to continue the campaign was fruitless, I'd want to make some public statement like, "How can you voters be so stupid to vote for this bum I've been running against? He's a liar and a cheat, and his mother wears combat boots! There, I said it. It needed to be said, and I said it. They're probably a petite size 6, but they're still combat boots!"

You have to have skin as thick and callous as the stones in a New Hampshire wall to withstand the offensive of a political campaign. These people are as compassionate as a roto-tiller when building themselves up and tearing their opponent down. An industrial meat grinder has greater empathy.

A typical exchange might be:

Candidate A: "My opponent's record is clear, he (she—it doesn't matter) has been in favor of every tax hike ever brought before him (her)."

Candidate B: "Candidate A doesn't clearly understand my record. I have never been in favor of a tax hike, but he (she) has always favored more taxes, especially taxes on blue-collar workers." Here I'd like to note that I'm not clear on just what a blue-collar worker is. I think it denotes someone who works for a living, but the only blue collar I have is on a shirt that would cause Janet to kill me if I wore it for work. My T-shirts don't have any collar, so I'm not sure where that leaves me in this discussion. My shirt with a blue collar, the whole shirt is blue; I usually wear it to hear a candidate speak.

Candidate A: "Candidate B has always favored taxes on the poor and elderly, and he cheats on his income tax."

Candidate B: "My worthy opponent and good friend (oh yeah), who wants to tax elementary school children, paid less tax than his secretary and lied about my record!"

Candidate A: "Candidate B approved a tax on handicapped kindergartners, dodged the draft, and has illegal aliens doing his (her) laundry!"

Candidate C: "I saw them both shopping for combat boots—petite size 6!"

I've strayed some from Maggie's song. I drove home, alone as I mentioned, with a plan to return after dark and find my dog—if she was still my dog. She might have been official Boy Scout property by then. Of course, while Maggie might be welcomed by young Scouts, I was certain that the Scout leaders would be more than happy to have one less disorderly creature adding to the mayhem.

I fixed a tire on the Oliver and weeded a couple of rows of carrots, and after dark, I went back to retrieve, or try to retrieve, my dog—whoever's dog. At this stage of Maggie's life, it was more a question of semantics as to whose dog she was. I paid the town dog tax. I think I fed her because she ate regularly at the farm, but who knows what else or where else she ate. Rudy could claim coownership, I suppose, as could Jim Falconer and others in town and out of town. I don't think anyone else was about to stumble around a Boy Scout campground to reclaim her, so I guess she was my dog. If I thought there might be anyone interested in adoption, however …

A couple of streetlights in the parking lot and the flickering glow from several campfires were the extent of the lighting at the town park, and the curling smoke from the campfires kept only the most timid of mosquitoes at bay. It would take more than a little smoke to keep a well-fed, mature New Hampshire mosquito from his appointed rounds. I noticed a fire truck parked near the ball field that I didn't think had been there earlier in the day. Maybe the Scouts were having fire-extinguishing practice, or the fire chief might have thought it wise to have a truck on hand in case a campfire became a bonfire. In any event, I went as directly as possible through the maze of tents and fires to the Scout leader's tent to find him as I had left him, plugged into the grass at his feet, captured in the silence of his headphones. "She's still here, I think," he told me. "She was at the big campfire near second base. They had some s'mores going over there. She wasn't into the sweets too much, but one of the kids had a jar of peanut butter, and she was enjoying that with graham crackers. I told them you'd be back for the dog and to keep her nearby."

True to his title, the Scout leader led the way to the second-base campfire, where we found no dog. We were told that she went to the home plate campfire for—oh, boy—hot dogs and beans. I'd lived the Maggie-full-of-baked-beans experience before and could only hope that she wasn't to be a guest in someone's pup tent. Maggie, beans, and a confined space could be a noxious combination. At home plate, they didn't know where she'd gone, but she was wearing Brentwood colors.

"What are Brentwood colors?" I asked.

"Green and white," the Scout leader told me. "The Scout's neckerchiefs are a different color for each town, and Brentwood's is green and white. They're in center field."

"And why would my dog be wearing Brentwood col ...? Oh, never mind." I knew how my dog was wearing Brentwood colors.

Center field produced only some giggling laughter from inside one of the tents, but everyone surrounding the campfire gave a straight-faced "She was here, but we don't know where she went." I was suspect with regard to the giggling in the tent, so I called a halfhearted "Maggie!" that went unanswered. The giggling stopped.

The Scout leader said that it was time for lights out and I'd have to continue looking for the dog the next day, so for the third time that day, I solemnly went home without a dog. Not too solemn, being aware of the baked beans that Maggie had eaten. She and her digestive tract wouldn't be welcome in anyone's tent.

The clock on my nightstand was showing 1:30 a.m. when I heard Maggie's seven-metered bark in the cornfield. She was an unwelcomed visitor for the raccoons that night, clad, I was sure, in a green and white Boy Scout neckerchief. The raccoons had more than bad luck to blame. They should have blamed a legume for having their evening meal disrupted because I'm sure it was the beans that drove her out of a warm tent and into the cornfield.

VERSE 13

OUR FARMHOUSE WAS BUILT, ACCORDING TO KENSINGTON'S published history, in 1743 and was constructed using the best methods of the time, given the scarcity of nails and Simpson metal connectors, in a post and beam manner. A good way to build a house, but it leaves the old place with a penchant to moan and groan. It's the consequence of those loose-fitting, pegged mortise and tendons. The connections slip a little when the wind pushes against it, and wood rubbing on wood gives a little groaning sound. I love my old house; I've lived here since I was three years old and hardly know any other, and I've grown accustomed to the occasional windy night murmurings. Probably, waking within the same walls for nearly all of my life has only served to make Dave a dull boy, but life is what it is, according to my favorite professional football coach. Janet had lived here only forty years or so and wasn't quite as indifferent to the house as I was when the wind blew. There are always other sounds, familiar sounds during the day that mask the house's whispers. But at night, when all else is still, you can hear the house communicating with itself.

I think that our worthy candidates become a little resistant to the murmurings of the electorate after a time but do so at their own peril. When their own voice becomes louder than the voices in the crowd, they keep saying what they want to say and stop hearing what they need to hear.

Janet woke me one night with, "Dave, there's a sound in the house."

"Of course there's a sound in the house. There's always a sound in the house." And I rolled over, doing my best imitation of a husband going back to sleep, although I knew from experience that sleep wasn't in my near future.

"It's not the usual sound!" she said. "It's different. It sounds like someone talking."

"Maybe it is someone talking," I said. "Maybe one of the neighbors is out for a walk on the road and is talking to themselves. Maybe Jim's out looking for his slippers. You know, calling them. 'Here, slipper, slipper, slipper.'"

"Listen!" she said.

I started to explain how the construction of the house—those old wood connections—squeak a little when the wind shifts their position, hoping that my dull muttering would bore her back to sleep, but that wasn't going to happen.

She put her hand over my mouth. Actually, it was dark as pitch in the bedroom, and she put her hand over my nose and right ear, but her point came across. I was to shut up and listen!

And there was a sound! A sound that wasn't supposed to be there. It seemed to be coming from the living room downstairs, and it sounded like someone talking! Talking quite loudly at that. They were making no attempt to speak in hushed tones; they were jabbering away like it was a filibuster.

"Maybe you should go have a look!" I suggested.

Janet gestured something in the dark that I didn't have to see to understand, so I swung my feet to the floor, dressed as usual in a pair of shorts. Not really the statement I wanted to make when confronting unwanted houseguests. I made a mental note to consider getting something to wear to bed that made me appear a little more sinister, maybe some military-looking camouflaged shorts. In the process of getting out of bed, I was also successful in knocking the lamp off the nightstand, thinking what a little noise might suggest to a burglar, if it was a burglar, that this would be a good time for them to leave the house.

"Be careful," my wife suggested. "You don't know what's down there."

"Maggie's down there," I said. "If it's a burglar, she'll chase them out."

"If it's a burglar," Janet said in a deafening whisper, "she'll lead them to Aunt Minnie's silver service and show them where we hide cash in the cookie jar!"

Janet was right; she would do that, thinking she'd get some cookies. The silver service is a family heirloom that in all probability is some plated alloy that was made in China, and the cookies in the jar have greater value than the cash. I thought to also look in the cookie jar after confronting our unknown guests, assuming they'd quickly leave. A fresh cookie would go a long way in suppressing my present anxieties.

Maggie hadn't made a sound, and I started to think that she was not at home but gossiping with Chief Aquilina near the old brick school on Route 150. Where's a big yellow dog when you really need one? She wasn't much of a barker. She'd bark mostly in greeting and seldom if ever in warning, but when she did bark, it was always the same seven beats. Seven even beats of "Woo-woo-woo-woo-woo-woo-woo!" It never varied. There was never a single "woo" or multiple "woos" of less or more than seven. The woos were of equal length and volume and as similar to one another and predictable as a stump speech.

Seven has a lot of alternate meanings in our society. There are deadly sins, brothers and their brides, seas, sons, days of creation, even dwarves, and I could add to that list the number of times Harold Stassen ran for president, but to us, the significance was Maggie's familiar bark. It was a rich, mellow sound, not the sharp, insistent, irritating yap of a lapdog—more the bay of a hound. It was also distinctive. We never had to ask, "What was that sound?" or "Which dog is that?" We knew Maggie's bark when we heard it.

There was the time that I was painting a side of the house. Our house is a confused combination of colonial and post-colonial additions, one attached to another in an apparent irreconcilable manner that all eventually reconciles itself. Woodsheds that became back storage rooms that became summer kitchens that became family rooms. A sort of family tree of architecture. Because of its size and sprawl, I paint the place in annual stages—the north side this year, one of the west sides next year, and so on. It might take seven years to paint the whole place; I never took time to figure it out. This day, I was high on a ladder, concentrating on my work. I usually concentrate on what I'm doing, even simple, repetitive tasks like dragging a paint brush across a piece of wood. I think it speaks for my lack of ability to perform too many tasks at one time. I'm not a multitasker. I also had the pickup parked near the base of the ladder, the doors open, and the radio blaring the Patriots game when Maggie, fresh from chasing frogs in the pond and lying across the seat of the truck, sounded her seven-toned greeting.

Without turning to see what she was barking at, I said, "What's up, Margaret?" Doesn't everyone talk to their dog? And if you did talk to your dog, you wouldn't expect her to reply.

"I just stopped in to see if you and Janet would come to dinner on Friday. We're having some friends down from Alstead and would like you to join us."

I nearly fell off the ladder, not because I thought the dog was talking but because I didn't expect the Margaret who replied to be our neighbor Margaret Perry. There are times when one feels foolish and times when one feels very foolish.

I never heard Maggie bark when she was hunting, whether it be woodchucks in the field, raccoons in the corn, or frogs in the pond. Maybe, like me, she wasn't a multitasker, and the concentration required for killing didn't allow for con-joined barking. Our presidential candidates, I'm sure, all being A-type personalities, are capable of multi-multitasking. They would have to be in order to manage the myriad workings of their campaigns. But then, their campaign managers must have to coordinate the facets of the candidate's schedule both present and future, so they must be multi-multi-multitaskers.

There were seldom other sounds from Maggie. She was too mild tempered to growl. She wasn't food aggressive. If another dog or cat tried to take her food, she'd either keep eating with them or walk away, sometimes to Rudy Hede's or Jim Falconer's, to get an uninterrupted meal there. Kids could squeeze, push, pull, lean, or yank without her complaining, and if it got too rough, she'd leave. Only on one occasion did

I hear her emit another sound. A dreadful wail of sadness and loss.

Not all communication is verbal of course. Maggie's style of interaction was often by insinuation. If she wanted to have her ears scratched, she would first stand by the chair you were sitting in and look at you. If you didn't at least put a hand on her head, she gave a gentle nudge with her nose, then a firmer nudge if you still didn't catch on. If she still wasn't able to get your attention, she would place her two front legs and the upper half of her body in your lap. That always worked. She got her ears scratched. If you were sitting in the large, overstuffed chair in the living room and you teased her by not roughing her coat or scratching her ears, she was known to climb her whole body into your lap. Your lap wasn't all she would sit on; she was spread all over the chair, and you were crushed, gasping for air, into the chair back while your lower extremities were being compacted into the chair cushion. Getting her off was more difficult than getting her on. I've had to resort to threats. Serious threats like "No dog biscuits until you get off me!" I'm sure those words had no meaning to her, but if I spoke the words and gave a firm push at the same time, she'd get off.

I think of Richard Nixon communicating nonverbally when he stood, hunch shouldered, arms raised, and two extended fingers on each hand projecting a V for victory. Of course, I remember too his verbal communication. "I am not a crook!" Maybe I need to think over the whole Richard Nixon similarity a little more.

Getting back to the sounds coming from our living room, I don't believe in ghosts or spirits, so I ruled out that possibility. The presence of a spirit would, however, deftly explain

Maggie's silence. Dog's probably don't have an awareness of the presence of a ghost. Unlike humans, who irrationalize their way to a proper angst over the nonpresence of a nonbeing, a dog, lacking the creative mind of a person, would not likely get exorcised over a non-anything. If there was a ghost— and as I crept closer to the head of the stair, I was certain there wasn't, at least quite certain there wasn't—Maggie could be curled up on the couch with this specter floating above her head and not even know it was there. That didn't explain the sounds that I thought to be human speech, unless it was the ghost of a filibustering congressman.

Maggie's persistent travels—her being here then there— suggested ubiquitousness. Many times when we thought Maggie to be here, she was there. She would appear from the barn when we were sure she was in the house, or from the field when we were sure she was in the barn. Or she would appear in the police cruiser … only too often. Making one of her magical appearances, into the back seat of his car when the doors were closed, Howdy once called her "O Ghost Who Drools."

In spite of my greatest effort to step softly, each stair tread complained like a distressed chicken as I lowered myself carefully toward the living room. If I had only stayed with the diet Janet had proposed … Technically, I would have had to actually start the diet Janet had proposed to effectively stay on the diet. In any case, a little less weight on the stairs would have produced a little less noise, better allowing me to sneak up on the maker of the sounds. I gained the bottom of the stair without incident. The sound continued from the living room—definitely human speech. I was only feet away from the source. Odd that the discussion was about the quality of a set of knives—probably the weapon of choice for who I now was certain were home invaders. Where was that stupid dog? Odd also that the knives they were discussing could cleanly slice an overripe tomato.

I hesitated only a moment longer while considering my approach. Should I retreat back up the stairs and call the police? Chief Aquilina was probably just at the end of the road, on Route 150, arresting my dog. The dog that should have been here protecting the farm. But if Mike was just that short distance away, he could be here quickly. Then again, this was my house. Even in shorts, I was lord of my castle. These people had entered my domain, and I should take care of this matter myself.

I took several deep breaths, braced my bare feet against the pine floor, and propelled myself through the doorway and into the living room. There was no one in the room but the cat stretched out on the couch and Maggie posing as an Egyptian cat goddess on the overstuffed chair, muzzle pointed heavenward, the TV remote under one of her outsized feet, for all the world watching a cutlery commercial. When I had gone upstairs to bed, apparently I'd left the remote where I was seated, and Maggie climbed into the chair a few hours later and when stepping on the remote had turned on the TV.

I snatched the remote from under her foot, accidently pressing the plastic catch that opened the little cover to the battery compartment, spraying rolling batteries like scratch corn for the chickens across the living room floor, with at least one rolling under the couch. Now I couldn't turn the blasted, blasting TV off. I knew there was a button on the TV set that would turn it off, but following years of disuse (I live by the remote—mute, fast-forward through commercials, replay the Patriots first down—the greatest invention since the cushioned tractor seat), I'd forgotten just which button it was. The first button I pressed increased the volume to a level that would wake a senator sleeping through a session on farm subsidies. The next button I pressed changed the channel to an exercise demonstration by three very attractive young ladies fitted into close-fitting shorts and tank tops. I hesitated in my search for the Off button just long enough for Janet to come down the stairs and ask in a somber voice if I found the source of the sounds that had driven me from my warm bed. In my panic to change the channel, I pushed the stupid volume increase button again, and one of the svelte exercisers said in a now too loud voice, "And tighten your buttocks like this while bending your …" at which time Janet reached past me and with one deft push of a finger stopped the commentary, darkened the screen, and darkened the room. I was relieved to be helped from my predicament yet at the same time disappointed not to find out what body part was to bend.

Janet turned on the lamp but not before I stepped on one of the dislodged batteries, driving a shot of pain through the bottom of my foot, clear up to the base of my skull. I hobbled around looking for a place to sit, but Janet had taken the parlor chair, Maggie was still reclined like a sovereign on the wing-back chair, and the cat was stretched out in the middle of the couch. I reached to move Pete, but he took a fully clawed swipe at my hand, adding to the other scars he'd put on my hand over the years. I glared at Maggie, but she inclined her head to look away, assuming that if she ignored me, I wasn't there. I went back up the stairs to bed.

VERSE 14

OUR FRIEND CHARLIE IS AN AMAZING MIX OF UNCOMPROMIS-
ing, perfectionist cabinet maker and charming, cheerful,
laughing, lighthearted humorist. He has an accent for every
story and a story for every accent. He'll tell one story sounding like a sardine-loving uncle from Norway (Noor-vey) and
the next about a female Russian tractor driver named Oof-ka.
His workmanship with wood is legend, and he always gets
the most enjoyment from the most difficult. He never met a
challenge that didn't plague him into new heights of perfection. From his shop, located in a renovated barn here on the
farm, he produces an astonishingly unique variety of cabinets,
desks, doors, and museum-quality boxes and containers of all
shapes and sizes. He once made a (departed) friend's coffin.

Though his gift with wood is what sun is to a crop of corn,
his gift with humor is like the whole growing season. Life
just wouldn't be the same without it. If Howdy was thunder,
Charlie is lightning. There is a static charge that emanates
from him all the time; a joke about the sun, a pun about the
rain; an anecdote about the latest news, a funny narrative
about our latest hot candidate. Always predictable and always funny, once I sat with him during part of a hospital stay
because of a tick bite. His blood pressure was so low that the

hospital staff was concerned for his life, but he had me laughing so hard with a continuous rambling about doctors, nurses, and hospitals that it made my stomach hurt. Nurse Cratchit would look into the room occasionally and glare at me with a perfect "Why don't you leave" look.

Charlie is the product of a boy who ran away from home at fifteen, who married too young, had a tragic divorce, and was separated from his two beautiful daughters, by a bitter wife, from their early childhood until their late teens. It was our good fortune to be part of his life when he was reunited with his girls, and we've been able to share his joy of fatherhood and now grandfatherhood. He could have been scarred by life's tragedies, but like a good oak tree, a few harsh winters make the grain straight and strong. There's not a bitter or pessimistic bone in his body or a harsh thought in his mind. One dreary November day, he said to me with a smile, "Just think. In only six weeks, the days will start getting longer!"

When I grumbled that there was a lot of cold weather between now and the shortest day, he said, "There you go. My calendar is half-full, and your thermometer is half-empty."

I'm still thinking about that. It's either a most astute thought, or it means nothing whatsoever. It's probably genius, and I just don't recognize it.

Charlie was one of Maggie's closet friends. Granted, in her eyes, he probably didn't have the gravitas of the pigs, but she appreciated his sense of humor, and he could give her a good scratch around the ears, which the pigs were not entirely trusted to do. He was as physically fit as a young fisher cat and loved riding his mountain bike or taking to the roads on Rollerblades, and he also enjoyed running with Maggie through the field like two laughing children. Maggie didn't laugh, but her joy was apparent with every step, and Charlie more than made up for what Maggie didn't say.

Charlie's shop was a cool, cement-floored retreat for Maggie during the summer and a soft, sawdust-lined, warm bed in the winter. Maggie always had a bad case of being on the wrong side of the door, so I'm sure Charlie spent more time opening and closing, opening and closing than he liked, but if he wanted Maggie's company, that's what he had to do. Maggie greeted Charlie when he arrived at 7:00 a.m. She'd go into the shop with him for twenty minutes, then go out and continue her farm duties (chasing, marking, snooping, barking), until midmorning and join Charlie for his coffee break. Charlie liked muffins; Maggie liked muffins. She'd tour the farm until noon and join Charlie for—what else? Lunch! A nap after lunch was just the thing, until three or so. Then back to the farm chores.

VERSE 15

OUR CAT PETE WAS A LESSON IN BELIEF. BELIEVE WHEN YOUR husband says it's a catbird. Early one summer morning, more than too many years ago, we awoke to the sound of a catbird coming from the trees opposite our farmhouse.

"I hear a cat across the road," Janet said.

"It's a catbird," I said. Sure, it might have been a real cat, but I wanted it to be a catbird. I really wanted it to be a catbird. A catbird would fly away, but a cat, which can't fly, though I wish they could, had a great likelihood of staying on the farm. We have a history of stray animals that stop straying when they've wandered as far as Moulton Ridge Road. No matter how much we feed them, they never leave.

Our discussion continued, and so did the cries of the catbird. In truth, the catbird kept getting louder by the minute until Janet left the bed and dressed, announcing that she'd investigate. She didn't trust that when I said I'd go look, my investigation would be thorough. At best, I'd walk up the road and have my attention diverted by almost anything but the catbird. That I'd let my attention be diverted was really at the heart of her belief. She thought I'd take a leisurely walk, more attendant to our crops growing on our side of the road than to the trees holding the catbird in the tree line opposite.

Janet walked, she found, she conquered. "He was halfway up the tree," she said, holding the weeks-old black-and-white kitten, "and when I held out my arms and called to him, he came straight down and let me lift him off the lower limb."

"If you put him back, his owners will find him and take him home," I said. "If you keep him here, they won't know where to look for him."

I got the look that didn't require words; I'd lost the discussion before it started. The cat was here—and here to stay.

That afternoon, our daughter Kelly stopped in to say hello and fell in love with the kitten. My reply was "Well, sure!" when she asked if she could take him home. I never thought it would be that easy! What a grand event this was. The cat wasn't even here a day. I was as elated as a candidate at the top of the Gallup poll. On the same day, I picked our first picking of string beans and found our pumpkin crop free of cucumber beetle. I was on a roll. Now if I only had a Megabucks ticket; it was that kind of day.

Three days later, my world collapsed. My back hurt from picking beans, there were little striped beetles on the pumpkins, and the cat was back. Kelly was renting a small house in Exeter, and the cat had started to destroy it. In Kelly's own words, "He used up my security deposit!"

On the first day, he shredded the wall-to-wall carpet in her living room. On the second day, he dismantled the curtains in the bedroom, and this was day three. He had started clawing the door casing in the kitchen when she put him in the car and brought him back to the farm.

I looked to Janet for some assurance that this was some kind of joke, but all she said was, "By the way, Dave, we've named him Repeat." The original Pete was a cat brought to us by our son Nate and had gone on to greater glory a couple of years back. While he was with us, he was one of those animals that was always in your face or under your feet. If you sat in a chair, he'd jump on your lap. If you walked through a doorway, he had to go through the opening either ahead of you or at the same time. He was known to climb onto the backs of our strawberry pickers while they were hunched over the rows of berries and perch like a raven on their shoulder while digging in with his claws to keep from falling. He was pretty unpopular. We're always saddened by the loss of our animals, but I wasn't too pained when Pete went to my final reward. And now we had a replacement?

It took a very short time for Repeat to become Pete. He settled into the farm like a conquering general—there to rule as he wished.

My hopes brightened a few days later when our son Tim told us that his girlfriend would like the kitten. "He's a wonderful cat! What he needs is a good home" I told them both as they stood waiting for my approval for the exchange. Exchange isn't the right word. I didn't want anything in exchange for the cat unless it was a promise to never return him.

As it turned out, I should have gotten that promise or some surety that I'd never see the cat again. A few days later, Tim had the temerity to break up with that wonderful, caring girl, and at midnight that same evening, a car stopped in front of the farm, a car door opened and slammed shut, and with a squeal of tires and a spray of gravel, continued on its way into the night. When I opened the front door to investigate, Pete rubbed against my leg as he walked in, never to leave for more than twenty years.

We don't have royalty in our country. Our founding fathers (and mothers) set to words the structure of our government, and they clearly stated that we would be presided over by a duly elected body with a president of our choice. It's a system that has some flaws, but to quote Winston Churchill, "Democracy is the worst form of government except for all the rest." We all would like to make some changes in our arrangement, but the outstanding majority believes in our right to choose our leaders.

Pete didn't get the message. We lower-form humans were here on the planet to serve him as he so richly deserved.

A week later, I wanted to rename him Rambo. Pete was a mighty and not loving warrior. Of all the domesticated animals, the cat is surely the closest in behavior to his natural ancestors. House cats took just a few tentative steps down the evolutionary path and moved off into the jungle to the nearest human environment, there to scratch and claw their way into human society. Dogs are as much like wolves, as a presidential primary is to the election of the sixth-grade president at the Kensington Elementary School (a fine institution of learning, by the way). Picture a hungry gray wolf and then picture a Chihuahua. See what I mean? Now the civilized cat, on the other hand—and I'm not certain that any cat is truly civilized—is a lot more like the original. I know, you have this image of Tabby in your mind, and on the other half of your personal split screen is a Bengal tiger, and you're thinking Dave may not have all his ducks in a line, but look at it from the perspective of a mouse: he's as dead no matter which one he woke up from a nap.

Now to get back to Pete—who was forever Pete, my name for him. Rambo never stuck. Pete was much closer to the original than any house cat I ever knew. Think again of the Chihuahua. Then picture the same dog cowering on the lower branches of a tree with a savage black-and-white cat glaring up at him from the ground. Take it a step further. Make it a little bigger than a Chihuahua. Think of a cocker spaniel or a good-sized border collie. We think of these as relaxed, civilized dogs, but I'm certain that neither one would dare cross Pete.

Pete weighed in at just under twenty pounds, and he was a slasher and a hunter. Hunter isn't the right word; hunters are engaged in a competition of survival. Pete was a slasher and a killer. He lived to kill—anything. Squirrels, rabbits, chipmunks, any rodent actually, skunks (young or adult), and any bird dumb enough to be so close that he could capture it. For the twenty-plus years that Pete was with us, we couldn't have a wild bird feeder; it would become a cat feeder, with remnant feathers on the ground beneath resembling a pillow fight. Like any serial killer, Pete liked to display his trophies. There was an unlimited supply of mouse heads, squirrel tails, and multicolored feathers on the lawn near the back door. One time, there were four gray squirrel tails arranged in near perfect pinwheel array near the base of the biggest maple tree along the fence line. I think he put them there as a warning to other tree-climbing trespassers that they were in Pete's kill zone. Janet and I saw him one spring day nearly a mile from the farm with a very dead chipmunk on his teeth. We assumed that he had to travel that distance to find game because he'd eliminated all other creatures within that one-mile radius.

By slasher, I mean that his four feet, claws attached, were active weapons. Anyone who touched the cat was most apt to get scratched. Any child who entered our house for the first time was told not to touch, bother, or try to pat Pete. "He will scratch you!" Not "He might scratch you," or "There is a possibility you'll be scratched." *"He will scratch you!"*

On countless occasions, we've heard the following conversation from a child who was out of sight but who had obviously found the black-and-white cat. "What a nice kitty. He's a soft kitty. He likes to be patted. He's purring. This kitty likes me." Too soon followed by "Waaaaaaaaa!" when Pete's true colors showed through and he drew first blood. The back of my own right hand looks like a scar tissue road map of Lithuania from the many clawings I received from Pete. Most attempts to pat him, move him, or just nudge him out of the way resulted in a lightning strike of his claws. He'd jump onto my lap, curl into a cat-shaped ball, and wait for me to move him. As soon as I gave him the slightest nudge, his four feet would recoil around my hand, and I'd suffer a scratch.

He loved the comforts of the house; he wasn't a barn cat. Picture a commando who likes his feather bed. But most of all, he loved … me! And I'm not a cat person. I'm sure that's why Pete liked me, because he understood that I didn't like him. I wouldn't threaten or harm a cat for any reason (well, maybe threaten), but I'm a dog guy. Of course, the elemental question is, why did we keep Pete? Why give a home to a monomani-acal cat? I offer our daughter and our son's girlfriend as two tokens of proof that no one else would take him. We could have performed the time-tested option of dropping him off at some unsuspecting farm, but that had apparently been done to him once, and for all I knew, he'd find his way back to us.

Pete's favorite comfort on a cold winter's evening was to climb into my lap and, after much positioning and reposition-ing, lie on his back with one paw, claws partially extended, pushed into my beard. If I moved at all, he'd further extend his claws until, like a threat, they'd just touched my skin. I haven't shaved my beard for thirty years (there is one exception, but that's a story unto itself), so I don't know if it's covering hidden scar tissue, but I can believe that it is.

Our friend Howdy didn't like cats. He didn't have an al-lergy; he had revulsion to cats. He couldn't tolerate any cat, and Pete knew it. He wouldn't leave Howdy alone. As soon as Howdy arrived at the farm, Pete would come out from wherever he'd been, either sleeping or killing—it was one or the other—and meander, feigning disinterest in the general direction of our friend. He would rub lightly against Howdy's leg or threaten to climb into his lap or just stare fixedly at him like an inquisitor mentally selecting a torture. *Let me see, the rack? No, we did that yesterday. Maybe the iron maiden.* One time while we were just standing in our dining room talking, Pete climbed to the top of an old pie safe we have and stepped boldly where no cat has gone before, directly onto Howdy's large, accommodating shoulder. The reaction was four things—immediate, predictable, fierce, and very satisfying to Pete. Howdy jumped as high as a four-hundred-pound man can jump while throwing his arms in the air like trees in a hurricane, all the while Pete rode his shoulder like a bull rider until he timed a smooth, effortless cat leap onto the harvest table and strutted, tail erect, into the next room before the rest of us had the time to react. Howdy stood quaking like a candidate who'd botched a practiced debate question, color drained from his face, looking like he'd just met Typhoid Mary.

There are many connotations that accompany the phrase *fellow traveler*. As friends who seemed like-minded, I always thought of my friends Charlie and Howdy as fellow travelers. Janet and I have been fellow travelers for forty years. I suppose presidential and vice presidential candidates are certainly fellow travelers until they reach the White House, when the president usually travels in his own direction, leaving the vice president to travel in circles or marking time until he's taken out and dusted off for another election. But when I refer to Pete as our fellow traveler, I mean more in the mobile/pragmatic sense. Pete often traveled with us. Janet and I walk a couple of miles each day, and Pete, along with the dogs, goes with us the entire distance, whether on the road or through the woods and fields, unless he's diverted by the prospect of dispatching some innocent animal unfortunate enough to come within the cat's kill zone. He cross-country skis with us in the winter. He does his best to hitchhike on the back of one of our skis and to go where we go. He usually tires of skiing before we go too far, but when we walk, he's usually there at the end with the rest of us.

VERSE 16

GREG AND LYNNE HOLMES ARE OUR NEIGHBORS TO THE west. They live in a cozy, well-maintained, colonial cape that may be the oldest house in Kensington. Like other older homes in New England that were built before the road leading to it was no more than a rutted path, it is situated closer to the road then would be desirable today, but that does nothing to take away from its charm. In fact, it adds to it. But my story has little to do with the front of their house and its proximity to the road. My story has to do with what's in back of their house. The Holmes have a crystal-clear, covered-in-the-winter, cool, inviting, and well-used-in-the-summer swimming pool. There are a few different kinds of pools, each varying in its construction. There are plastic wading pools, above-ground pools, concrete pools, and pools whose shape is molded in sand, and then a plastic liner is placed over the sand, and the shape is maintained by the weight of the water captured in the plastic liner. The Holmes' pool is the latter—an attractive, in-ground pool lined with a heavy, durable plastic.

Their pool has a removable set of stairs at the shallow end that allows a swimmer to walk out of the pool as gracefully as a movie star, and there's a ladder at the deep end that gives an exit to the more athletic, swimming champ type. In late spring, the Holmes had removed the cover from their pool and added some chemicals to clear the water of various algae growths but hadn't as yet installed the removable stair. The only way out of the pool was by means of the deep end ladder.

Occasionally, a presidential candidate will get himself into a state of affairs that's difficult to escape. When running for president in 1987, Gary Hart invited the press to follow him around and "be very bored." They followed him to his yacht, the *Monkey Business,* docked in Miami, and found him involved with an attractive blonde who was not his wife.

Not that day or any day since has anyone had any idea why Maggie jumped into the Holmes' pool, whether to cool off, chase frogs, or because it was there. Whatever the reason, she did jump in—and at such a time that none of the Holmes were home. She paddled around for no one knows how long, because no one knew when she jumped in. One can assume she was in the pool for some time because there was ample evidence that she made many efforts to remove herself from the pool. Her technique for escape was to place her front paws on the upper edge of the pool and try to pull herself up and out by pulling with her front legs and a little running in place with her back legs trying to gain purchase against the plastic liner—that was ripped into shreds by the claws in her back feet. She was scrambling like Gary Hart trying to get out of his yacht without shredding to confetti all that supported him.

The turkey buzzards were circling by the time Greg came home to find a waterlogged dog in his pool, and he was understandably torn between relief that his neighbor's dog hadn't drown and wanting to drown her for ruining his pool liner. Maggie, for her part, demonstrated her gratitude for the assistance by immediately jumping up on her savior and nearly pushing him into his own pool. She trotted home, stopping for a drink at our pond before she placed her soggy body on the couch for a ten-hour nap.

VERSE 17

MAGGIE COULD ABIDE ANY CALAMITY BUT COULD NOT BEAR thunder, fireworks, or gunshots. The Fourth of July and hunting season were unhappy times for her—omnipresent fireworks on Independence Day, and for the six weeks of hunting season, every hunter firing twenty shots, maybe more, for every hit (kind of like the excess verbiage from a presidential campaign), making the air alive with gunshots. Sunday morning brought them all out, the experienced and the novice. You could identify the two easily by their dress—the novices with their shotguns at port arms, looking like they had just left a week's pay at L. L. Bean, and the old natives slouching along, dressed in faded red jackets, their firearms slung casually over their shoulders the way you'd carry a pitchfork into a hay field.

As I've written, Janet and I enjoy walking, and our animals walk with us usually. It was a sparkling Sunday morning during primary and hunting season. The two are not mutually exclusive though similar in their avarice. We were about to start west on Moulton Ridge Road when a newbie hunter, brightly garbed in John Kerry scarlet as radiant as the morning, stepped his new Italian hunting boots into our drive and asked through a smile worthy of a candidate on voting day, "Do you mind if I shoot the goose that's in your pond?"

I wasn't aware that there was a goose in our pond but said, "Well, yeah, I guess I do mind. I don't know that you're supposed to shoot geese in the water anyway. I think they're supposed to be in flight." I didn't know the goose-shooting rules, but blasting away at a body of water didn't seem fair—at least for the geese. I don't know if it was the sight of bright scarlet that attracted her or the smell of new scarlet, but Maggie gave the goose hunter an earnest goose with her curious nose, and with a sudden intake of breath like that brought on by a ten-point drop in the polls, he muttered something unintelligible and continued on his way. Probably to find another goose on another pond—a pond that didn't have a big dog with a rather pointed nose.

We often had Canada geese in our pond, but we started our walk that morning by going to see the reported goose anyway, Maggie taking the lead. At the pond, she eased herself into the water and, true to canine form, dogpaddled after the dozen or so geese in the water. They swam efficiently away, their backs turned, almost ignoring her, and moved into a small growth of alders on the far bank. Maggie followed jerkily along, her nose a small periscope stretching out of the water. When she was a few yards from the birds, they nonchalantly, like partisan parties, split into two groups and moved easily and silently as ghosts to opposite ends of the pond, there to peck at bits of floating vegetation, waiting to see which party, if either, the water-soaked dog would follow. She turned and labored after one group until she was within a short distance, and then they did an effortless flanking maneuver and paddled lightly away. I felt sure that this play had taken place before—maybe rehearsed daily, the players certain of the others' stage direction and lines. Janet and I got bored with the performance and called the dog out of the water as we walked away. Minutes later, she splashed ashore and ran to catch up, not shaking herself dry until she stood between us, effectively making us as wet as she.

Janet and I walked along the road, but our animals, especially Maggie, took meandering routes that carried her through the woods, fields, and swamps that lined the road, adding about four miles of travel to our one. During her explorations, she accumulated pine needles, burrs, weeds, and weed seed in her coat like it was a department store of debris. Mud on aisle nine, burdock on aisle six with the milkweed seed, velvetleaf spore on her tail with bittersweet pods, and so on. She could best be described as a mess—a happy mess, but still …

We had walked along Moulton Ridge Road for a mile or more when Rudy, driving home from church in his car, stopped to ask if we still had sweet corn to sell. Like his lawn, Rudy takes great pride in his car. It's not an expensive luxury model, but it's a full-sized American make that he keeps waxed and spotless, inside and out. Maggie had her wet nose, caked with red clay from—well, I don't know where from, but it was there. Anyway, her clay-covered nose was reaching toward the car window, no doubt thinking that her pal Rudy had a little affection for her if not a dog treat. Rudy reached a tentative hand out to find and touch a dry spot on Maggie's clay-covered head when she backed up slightly. Our neighbor, determined to be a good neighbor and dog lover, opened the car door to better reach the retreating animal, but to his misfortune and the misfortune of his car's interior, at the same instant, a hunter, unseen but not a quarter mile away, fired his gun. The report launched Maggie through Rudy's open door, up and over Rudy's stooped back—and clean white shirt—and deposited her, shivering, shaking, and dripping in the previously, but no longer, spotless white upholstery of the passenger seat.

We were all speechless. There sat our dog, quaking, dripping, and drooling in our kindly neighbor's spotless car. Our kindly neighbor, his good suit and white shirt caked with red clay, milkweed spore, pine needles, and who knew what else, did his level best to remain a kindly neighbor, and Janet and I stood aghast at the actions of our dog. I don't know why, but Rudy, like the proverbial farmer who closed the barn door after the fact, closed the driver's door, and Janet ran around to the passenger door, the locked passenger door, and tried to open it and pull Maggie out. I called, "Maggie, Maggie, Maggie!" an admonishment, not a "come here" command, and had more luck than Janet trying to open the door. Maggie stepped across and jutted her head toward me out the open driver's side window. Of course, this placed her two filthy front feet in Rudy's lap—not a comfortable thing—her swamp-scented, dripping, matted body leaning against and soaking his jacket and tie. I grabbed the fur on the scruff of her neck and gave a pull, but she set the schedule, and she wasn't ready to leave the protection of Rudy's car. As I pulled, of course, it placed more weight on her front feet, increasing the pressure on Rudy's lap, and in the most polite phrasing Rudy could conceive, he suggested that I stop trying to pull the dog out through the window.

We were at an impasse, as deadlocked as Congress. Maggie

was firmly rooted in place. She wasn't about to leave the safety of the car and chance exposure to another gunshot. Janet couldn't open the passenger door, and Rudy couldn't reach across the seat and unlock it. The more I pulled, the more uncomfortable Rudy became, and so for a full minute, we all stayed in place.

Exasperated, Rudy said, "Let me give you the keys, and Janet can open the door, and maybe Maggie will go out that side."

A fine plan if I ever heard one. Rudy managed to reach around the dog, who by now was panting slightly, causing a rhythmic movement in her body and driving her paws into Rudy's lap, retrieve the keys from the ignition, and hand them to me through the open window. It was a fistful of devices, keys for the ignition and trunk, house keys, small padlock keys for who knows what, one of those badges that has the make of the car on it, a small flashlight, a membership card for the supermarket, even a tiny calculator. In my rush to get this enterprise under way, I dropped the keys with a clang and, when moving to pick them up, managed to kick them under the car. When the going gets tough, the tough can be really clumsy!

On hands and knees, I looked beneath the car and saw that the keys had fallen into one of Moulton Ridge's finer potholes. By flattening myself—not an easy task because I'm not very flat to start with—I was able to reach beneath the car but not far enough to reach the keys. While reaching for the keys, I noticed that Rudy wasn't the only one coming home from church. When he stopped to chat, he didn't bother to pull to the side of the road. The pavement is just wide enough for two cars to pass, so there isn't a side of the road as such.

When I looked first up and then down the road, I saw quite a contingent of worshipers in their cars, unable to pull past us, all anxious for Sunday dinner, wondering what was up with the Lambert family now. Probably not a few of those in waiting thinking that if the Lamberts had gone to church, this situation would have been avoided.

Maggie must have wondered what I was doing sprawled on the road because she leapt from the car window, and judging from his pained cry, causing Rudy some obvious discomfort, and landed those huge, muddy feet directly on my back, pushing all the air from my lungs. I gasped, Janet laughed, Rudy moaned, and Maggie pushed her clay-caked muzzle into my neck, trying to see what I was reaching for under the car.

After some stretching, straining, and a few generous grunts, I was able to grasp the key collection, extract myself from beneath Rudy's car, and give him his keys. He uttered a clipped goodbye, fumbled for the ignition key, started the car, and drove on, allowing one of the rare traffic jams on Moulton Ridge Road to break up and the jammers proceed home to dinner.

We continued our walk, Maggie, at least for the present, having forgotten the gunshots. I was hopeful that by now, nearing midday, the hunters would all be hungry and go home for lunch. I wondered how many would be having some delicacy of wild game, how many would be eating lunch meat sandwiches, and who would go to McDonald's. Maggie preceded us as we left the pavement and followed an abandoned road into the woods that would lead us eventually back to our own upper cornfield. Maggie couldn't abide by our dawdling pace, so she ran on ahead of us, crashing between the trees and through the brush with the delicacy of a Brahma bull.

The woods were as parched as a stone wall in a drought, each broken twig exploding like small cannon. Gray squirrels arching like serpents through the dry leaves made as much noise as a big yellow dog, and a big yellow dog created the din of a brown bear. The warm autumn sun painted dappled patterns through the falling leaves that were making a quilt of the forest floor. An invisible brace of cock pheasants played the hollow, whistled melody of a fall-afternoon symphony.

Janet and I shuffled along, kicking at an occasional pine cone and discussing the important matters of life, the price of carrots, the color of curtains for the family room, and new tractor tires. Well, I wanted to talk about new tractor tires, and Janet introduced curtain colors in an effort to direct me away from the discussion about new tractors tires—any tractor tires actually, new or old, large or small, round or flat. Her tactic of misdirection is flawless. I would say something like, "The back tires on the Oliver are starting to crack and show some wear. They are the original tires, so they're twenty-five years old or older, and I'd like to replace them this year."

To which she replied as though we'd been talking about curtains for the last hour, "My mother had green curtains in her kitchen. Do you remember them? I wouldn't want the family room curtains to be quite that dark, and I never cared for the pattern of hers, but I think a green like, like—like the leaf lettuce we grew this year—yes, the same as the leaf lettuce but hung like my mother's, with tabs that fit over wood dowels. You could make a small bracket that the dowels could fit into, couldn't you? I think my dad made hers, or maybe it was my brother, Buck. Do you remember?"

Now, there are numerous replies to the topic she introduced, like more talk about curtains, about which I know nothing, or the color green as it applies to leaf lettuce or even other green crops like brussels sprouts, but none of my replies can have anything to do with tractor tires. Her tack is as pure as a filibuster; she has the floor, the topic, and the entire audience of one, and the debate can't be changed. All I can do is talk about curtains—rather, listen about curtains.

So, listen about curtains I did, until Maggie came crashing through the woods with the stealth of a bull moose, running toward us, shaking her head violently and looking like Popeye's nemesis, Blutto. Her entire muzzle was covered with a dense beard of porcupine quills. I think she had more quills sticking into her than a good-sized porcupine would have sticking out of him—or her. I started to pull some out, but if you've ever pulled porcupine quills, you know it's not easy. Each quill has a row of barbs like tiny fishhooks on the end that make removal as difficult as getting a candidate to stop speaking in a debate. Maggie stood still and let me remove a few, but they protruded from the inside of her mouth and tongue and most of her face and nose, and it was more than I could deal with on the spot. I needed a pair of pliers.

By the time we hurried the mile home, my idea of trying to remove the quills by myself had become as lost in history as Teddy Roosevelt's running mate, so I called the vet, interrupting her from one of the last afternoons in her family's new pool. No doubt when I explained my problem, she started having visions of the latest technology in pool heaters that would extend the use of their pool by a few more afternoons, thanks to our contribution to her family's happiness.

Maggie didn't seem to experience any pain, though I can't imagine why not, but with a mouth full of quills, she couldn't close her mouth very well, and that contributed manyfold to her usual copious drool factor. On the way to the new vet's office (Bob Marston had retired), she sat on the truck seat beside me, her head alternating between turns to the passenger's window and leaning across me in an effort to block my vision and saturate my clothes with dog slaver.

A couple of hours later, with a bill in hand that reflected an emergency visit on Sunday afternoon, ensuring our veterinarian that her family now had sufficient funds for that new pool heater, squelching any thoughts of tractor tires, I returned to the farm with a dog seeming none the worse for a dose of anesthesia and a large injection of antibiotic. It must have been the remnants of anesthesia that caused her slobber to increase by a factor of ten, but increase it did, until the truck seat looked as it would in the wake of a flood. Back at the farm, she bounded from the truck as soon as I opened the door and disappeared around the farmhouse. I wanted to salvage something from the day, so, without another thought regarding Maggie's whereabouts, I turned to picking the last of the popcorn. I should not have been so blasé vis-à-vis the dog. I never use the phrase vis-à-vis, but then blasé is foreign to my speech, so when using one, it seems only natural to use the other. The point of this is that I shouldn't have disregarded the dog.

Some hours later, when I had picked my second tractor bucket full of popcorn and was bringing it from the field to husk and hang to dry, I saw the big yellow dog standing over a moderate-sized, dark shape on the lawn. I was afraid to investigate. It wasn't fear that deterred me from looking. It was the knowledge that Maggie was so savagely determined that she would do the unthinkable—finish the job she started earlier in the day. She went back into the woods and found the porcupine. Whether she had killed it earlier in the day or went back to finish it off, I don't know, but in either case, she brought the carcass home and proudly displayed it, like a kewpie doll won in a side show, on our front lawn. Of course, she had as many, if not more, quills as before, and of course removal required a second and rather embarrassing trip to the vet. She gave Maggie a little extra anesthesia this time, trying to keep her sedated through the evening—maybe long enough to forget in case there were other porcupine family members that she neglected to eradicate. The second bill of the day would extend the vet's pool season with a new and bigger pool heater.

I buried the dead porcupine in a deep hole to prevent Maggie from smelling it and digging it up. That was the last porcupine she tangled with. If there were others, she fought them without getting a single quill, and that wasn't Maggie's style.

VERSE 18

THATCHER HAD BEEN WITH US FOR TWELVE YEARS OR MORE, a birthday gift from our daughter Vicki. He was quiet, steady, and humble. He seldom barked because he didn't want to draw attention to himself. As I've said before, he was a herding dog, but we had only chickens to herd, and while he herded them with sincerity, his position on the farm was more honorary than operational. He preferred a supporting role, not even vice presidential, maybe more like minority whip or even minority suggester or minority follower.

He lived his life with a quiet reservation, occasionally traveling the fields and woodlot with Maggie but never *traveling* with Maggie, as only Maggie could travel. One warm autumn day, when he came to the end of his life with us, we were all saddened but none as disconsolate as Maggie. Her sonorous eulogy was as tragic as any voice I'd ever witnessed. She lay beside his still form and, starting at a low, nearly undetectable register, raised her face and voice upward to a throaty, mournful wail not unlike the wolves in her ancestry. Her cry went on for only minutes but seemed like hours. A beautiful elegy filled with primal sound and tones unheard in our own verbal mutterings. We humans have language and are supposed to be the planet's ultimate communicators. I've never heard any expression as complete or equal to Maggie's cry. Janet and I spoke not another word for the entire day. Maggie had said it all.

We all missed our herding dog, but none of us as much as Maggie. She became more of a quiet fixture at the farm, companionable with Janet and me but lacking her usual interest in going to Rudy Hede's or the Falconers'. Many nights, she slept on the front lawn, not wanting to come into the house but lacking the desire to perform a traffic study on Route 150 or find out if there was a ham and bean supper at the Congregational church. She went with me when I went to the field but would lie quietly beside the tractor or jump into the bed of the truck and sleep. She began to lose weight, and her luxurious coat, usually the color and sheen of a fresh honeycomb, was turning to the luster of old straw.

It was a year with a good harvest, and it continued through the blazing of the maples, the eventual drenching rain that dislodged the leaves from the hardwood trees, and then the first dusting of snow. Maggie was happy when the first flakes blew like floating white dust through the fields. She galloped across the yard but didn't dance her usual joyful pirouette. We took into account that she was getting older, maybe statelier, but we also understood she missed her friend Thatcher.

As was common, neighboring dogs came to the farm to visit with the canine matron, but, preferring to be alone, she would curl up on the front porch and, with a deep sigh, turn her back on local society. Our daughter Kelly owned a couple of Chinese Shar Peis that she would bring to the farm to run through the fields and get a little exercise. We hoped they might offer some companionship for Maggie, but though the wrinkly little dogs were friendly and eager to have Maggie join them in a jubilant romp in the faded corn, maybe find a woodchuck to torment or sneak up to Rudy's house—Rudy most always had snacks for Maggie and other neighborhood dogs—Maggie would go into the living room and lie quietly on the fireplace hearth and wait until her cousins had gone home. After a fashion, she'd amble through the house or go outside and keep her own company. Kelly was upset that she and her dogs couldn't bring Maggie out of her funk. None of us could.

I've stated before in this story, I'm a dog person. I've always had a dog. I can't remember a day without a dog, but I never consciously sought out a dog. I never went to the pound or a kennel and said, "I'd like to buy a dog." The dogs always came. We had a corgi named Skippy that my sisters brought home from the Grange Hall where they found her, the butt of pranksters with tin cans tied to her tail. During a snowstorm, my sister Betty found Lucky in a phone booth in Exeter. A beautiful, melodious, and terribly gun-shy old hound that we named Lady wandered into the farm during bird season one year and, to our benefit, never left. I know, you're thinking, *Dave, how about Maggie? She didn't just show up on your doorstep!* I still claim to be an innocent. Janet was the one who retrieved the "Free to a good home" puppy. Anyway, I don't want to slow down my story with technicalities. My lifetime of dogs simply arrived, and the same was true with Tucker.

It was a few days before Christmas, and we had some friends and relatives in for an informal party. Charlie was there entertaining everyone with his smooth humor. Howdy, attired in his one-of-a-kind reindeer hat complete with antlers, was happily tasting all of Janet's cooking. Janet's brother

Buck was competing with Howdy for the title of I Ate the Most! And Janet's cousin Shep came with his two children, his then girlfriend—now wife—with her two children and her behemoth of a dog named Goliath, or maybe it was a Goliath of a dog named Behemoth, but it was something like that. Maggie dispensed with her hostess chores as quickly and as perfunctorily as a teenager takes out the trash, gave Goliath/Behemoth a once-over sniff, and retired to the living room, leaving the remainder of the house to the remainder of the revelers. Charlie had gathered a small audience as he improvised a story, something about Santa's elves being subordinate clauses, when in the midst of the crush of guests, singers, servers, eaters, storytellers, laughing children, and large dogs, our daughter Kelly arrived with the phrase now indelible in Lambert family history, "Merry Christmas, Mom and Dave. Meet Tucker."

Please recall that Maggie was about six months old when she arrived and weighed sixty-five pounds. She was big. Tucker wasn't six months old yet but weighed nearer to eighty pounds. He was a registered Great Pyrenees who in his brief lifetime had outgrown one apartment family and was on his way to a farm family—us. That someone living in a small apartment would buy a puppy, knowing their ultimate size would be nearly that of a bear, seems a little inconsistent with reason. It's like New Hampshire hosting a presidential primary; our guests outgrow us after every fourth February. Maggie must have sensed the additional reveler, but Tucker didn't revel. He lay beneath the table in the family room and studied ankles. Queen Canine gave him a thorough nasaling, and she must have smelled something she liked because she joined him under the table but not before she hit Howdy up for the remaining half of his devilled egg. Howdy and Maggie had a history of eggs. The two dogs kept company for a while before Maggie returned to the living room. It was a modest beginning to a lasting friendship.

So, we rescued Tucker in the sense that we don't know where he would have gone had he not affixed himself here on Moulton Ridge Road. Not everyone has the facilities to take in and provide for these canine giants. I wasn't entirely sure that I wanted to play caregiver to a mountainous pile of ever-shedding fur, and though Kelly told us graciously that we didn't have to keep him—she could take him back to … well, who knows to what she'd take him back.

Now at least twelve Christmas gatherings have passed since Tucker's arrival, and he's gone from big to huge to old here on the farm. But this is Maggie's song, and I want to keep my story anchored to her time with us, though her story was as bound to Tucker's as it was to ours, for, you see, Tucker was an avid fellow traveler with Maggie. As he grew, and that was rapid growth, he took and he sprouted and he matured faster than winter rye. (Matured isn't the right word, for maturing isn't something Tucker did well.) And like a good grain crop, all his growing came to an eventual head.

Tucker traveled like Maggie, but he hadn't nearly her smarts. Tucker had no smarts at all—about anything. He knew where his food was, finding water wasn't a problem, and he'd sleep standing up, but his massive feet attached to those four long legs could take him a lot of miles in a very short time. But for every one of Maggie's smarts, Tucker had three stupids. Maggie traveled safely on the side of the road; Tucker walked in the middle. Maggie visited the neighbors, and Tucker ripped open their screen door, attempting to get into their house. Maggie marched in the Memorial Day parade, and Tucker removed the wreathes that the school kids put on the veterans' graves at the cemetery. Maggie would return from a day of visiting, and I'd have to drive the pickup to a complaining distant neighbor and retrieve Tucker. I'm sure he didn't know how to get home otherwise. Tucker was big, friendly, and handsome, but he couldn't spell potato.

While Maggie was a manageable problem, Tucker was not so manageable. Some contrary people in politics are referred to as a loose cannon; Tucker was a loose battleship. Something had to change. The first thing to change was a torn anterior cruciate ligament, better known by people who follows sports and athletes as a torn ACL. Tucker developed a severe limp, and our vet, after a little poking and pulling, followed by an x-ray, announced that she would now have enough money to put in that big in-ground swimming pool, replacing the above-ground pool that Maggie and the porcupine had helped finance. I had been accustomed to leaving a little petty cash at the vet's office, you know, kind of a "Well, I guess we'll go without ice cream for a couple of weeks." Not, "Well, I guess we'll go without making the mortgage payment for a year or two!" I didn't think an ACL repair for a human could cost that much, let alone a dog—a Christmas-present dog no less!

Tucker had to be restrained for six weeks following his surgery, and during this period, we discovered that life was more pleasant without having to continually wonder where the big, dumb dog might be. We knew where he was! He was either in the house or on his spiffy new dog run or being taken for a leisurely walk on a leash by one of his human slaves. We so enjoyed knowing where the village idiot was that we made a plan for a permanent solution to the travel problem. We installed an invisible dog fence.

The invisible fence consists of a wire buried a few inches in the ground along a closed perimeter where you wish to keep the animal confined. The dog wears a collar that emits a beeping sound when it nears the buried wire. After several beeps, the collar gives the dog a moderate shock, not a debilitating jolt, just a substantial tingle to remind the animal that when they hear the beeping, they should stop and not cross the buried wire. The success of the fence rests predominantly on a rigorous training period while you walk the dog, twice daily, just within the fence's perimeter, establishing in the dog's mind the new limits of their travel.

Janet and I had been walking a considerable distance each morning for years, so when we surrounded our twenty-acre field with the invisible fence, we altered our route from walking Moulton Ridge Road to the half mile or so of our fenced perimeter, it wasn't a big deal. Only now we walked Maggie on a leash (we walked Tucker on a leash when he was sufficiently healed from his surgery), and of course Pete went with us, going only as far as his first daily kill.

We enjoyed our new walk so much that we've continued it each day ever since. Sometimes on snowshoes and sometimes on cross-country skis, but without fail, each day finds us in rain, snow, or the dark of 5:30 a.m. with our animals, circling our field, listening to the wonderful sounds of early morning cupped in the wonderful quiet of early morning. No cars, car horns, tractors, phones, radio, or television; just the distressed cry of a small animal followed by the primal crunching of cat's teeth on pliant flesh.

It was maybe a month after Maggie was trained to the fence that I was driving by Rudy's house on the tractor and noticed that he had a new lawn ornament that looked appallingly like our dog Maggie. It was the same size and color. It was posed in a manner familiar to our dog, and it carried itself with the same less than regal attitude as our dog. I was just trying to get my head around the idea that Rudy missed Maggie so much that he got himself a concrete Maggie when his new lawn ornament wagged its tail.

Now, in terms of expense, the cost of the invisible fence was overshadowed by Tucker's ACL repair. Of course, the cost of new tires for the tractor would be overshadowed by Tucker's ACL repair, but that's not my point. We had achieved something greater than the ability to eke out the money for the invisible fence; we had achieved peace of mind! What, I ask, can give sweeter nurturance to heart and soul than peace of mind? Granted, giving someone a piece of your mind has a large portion of satisfaction attached to it, but to lie back in that soft bed of serenity, to take one's ease in the warm waters of security, only to be struck into awakening by the casual wagging of a tail. Why, if the brakes had worked on the tractor, I'd have stopped right there and taken some sort of firm—if not affirmative—action! Instead, I kept rolling on by, speechless but intent on finding out how, after weeks of training, many dollars of expense, and bushels of heaped-up hopes, Maggie defied technology and went back to her wandering ways.

I knew then how the losing candidates in our presidential primary feel the morning after the big day. There are two winners, a Democrat and a Republican, and a following sea of losers all feeling like I did after seeing Maggie on Rudy's lawn. We planted our seeds of knowledge and technology, spread our fertilizer of labor and travail, and reaped—failure! All our hopes were blown like chaff in the wind of destiny. Well, maybe not as bad as chaff in the wind of destiny, but still ...

A little later, when I came back by Rudy's, his lawn ornament rose from its sleep like an animated statue of Aphrodite and followed me home. When she reached the invisible barrier, she put her head down, and with the gritting of her canine jaws, Maggie with a small cry walked through the fence! I felt horrible! Maggie was so intent on continuing her neighborly visitations that she was willing to endure pain to do it.

Janet and I rationalized our way to confounding the issue by agreeing with the invisible fence people that to protect her from possible harm on the road, it would be in her best interest to increase the electric sensation from the collar in an attempt to keep her within the fence. The adjustment made, Maggie appeared to respect the new voltage and stayed within the confines of the twenty-acre field. She and Tucker roamed the field to the limits, chasing woodchucks and raccoons without altering traffic flow on Route 150 or spending time visiting the neighbors. In a few weeks, I began to think that all was right with the world. With Maggie's help, we harvested the last of the potatoes and carrots, and then we brought in the popcorn and brussels sprouts and put the fields to bed for the winter.

Janet was teaching a special education student at the farm; this was joy for Maggie and Tucker. Tucker was the eager playmate, running off his energy with the boy when he arrived in the morning and during his recess. Maggie, whose age was slowing her down, was content just to sit by the boy, have her ears scratched, and wait patiently to share his lunch. I spent most of my time cutting firewood or repairing farmstead and machines in anticipation of next season.

We became so accustomed to knowing the location of our two large dogs that we pretty much ignored them unless they were with us. That is, we didn't have to look for them; we knew that they were in the twenty-acre corral. Tucker, in an exuberant chase, followed an animal across the fence and into the woods on one occasion but stopped about twenty paces after he got a shock, then, like an undecided voter, sat in one spot and barked until I came to get him. I removed his collar as he crossed the line back into our field, then replaced it, and he hasn't left the farm since.

Presidential elections, the property tax bill, and winter are all most predictable, but their arrival always carries with them small surprise, like "I knew this was coming, but why'd it have to come so soon?" Rudy Hede, bundled up in his coat, hat, boots, gloves, and scarf, was trudging along Moulton Ridge Road on one of those first really cold days of winter, one of those days when all New Englanders ask themselves, "What am I doing here when there are warm places in the world?" and "Gee, it's been a long time since I visited my sister Sally in Florida!" Rudy saw me wound up in jumper cables, trying to start one of the Eisenhower-era tractors, and in a neighborly fashion stopped to inquire about our general health, if I was ready for winter, the disposition of our animals, and to remark how nice it was to see Maggie visiting around the neighborhood again.

I said that Janet and I were fine, that I was never ready for winter, that our animals were all in good and vigorous health and "What do you mean, about Maggie visiting the neighborhood?"

"Well," Rudy replied, "she comes for a visit nearly every day. In fact, she was in my living room and came out to walk with me just now, but I don't know where she made off to." Rudy and I both looked up the road in the direction he had traveled and didn't see the big yellow dog. We did, however, see her as she trotted around from the back of the barn, tail wagging and sporting her bright green, invisible-fence collar.

Maggie approached us like a candidate pandering for votes, uncertain who she should anoint first with her sodden feet. I guess she considered my grease-and-soil-infested jacket more appropriate, so she jumped on me in greeting and looked at Rudy with her wet tongue lolling out of her mouth, her huge, dripping paws resting on my shoulders. I noted that she had regained her weight and maybe a few pounds more.

"This collar is supposed to keep her on our land and off the road," I said, removing it from her neck. "Maybe it's not working." And with that pathetic bit of misinformation and collar in hand, I walked across the invisible fence. The hand holding the collar was jolted as if it was clamped onto an electric fence. The collar was working! I should have started casting about for solutions to a problem, but instead I felt saddened that I was subjecting our dog to what amounted to torture just to make her stay home. If, like Tucker, she was subdued into respecting the fence and didn't challenge it almost continuously, I wouldn't have felt as I did, but she was following her lifelong routine of traveling and visiting, and it didn't appear that I was about to change it. Once again, I called the invisible fence technician, who told me that the dog's collar was turned up as high as possible and that I should give her a little more time and maybe more training.

We spent another week or more, twice a day, walking Maggie around within the perimeter of the fence, attempting to train her to remain and refrain (from leaving the enclosure). Stay within and not without. Stay on the farm and out of harm. She was eager to go for the walks. She dutifully waited for the leash. She pranced and horsed around with Tucker and walked on the leash like a show dog. She was as proud as a candidate ahead in the polls. But for all the training, the walking, and encouragement, Maggie was still to be seen, almost daily, patrolling the neighborhood, at Rudy's house or the Falconer property. She didn't go far, but she was certainly not restricted by the fence.

Our farm pond feeds into a brook that passes beneath Moulton Ridge Road, a few hundred feet west of the farmhouse. In 1954, Hurricane Carol passed through the heart of New England, on a path bisecting New Hampshire, with nearly eighty-five-mile-per-hour winds and dumping more than eight inches of rain. Our small brook became a torrent, overflowing its banks and Moulton Ridge Road. There was a small, inadequate culvert that directed the brook beneath the road, but before the storm was half-over, the culvert and road overflowed, and a section of road twenty feet wide and twelve feet deep was removed and deposited downstream. After the storm, we could still travel east on Moulton Ridge Road, but unless you had a means of jumping over a twenty-foot ditch, you couldn't travel west.

Kensington is a small town that functions on a small budget, but after discussion among the town fathers worthy of a primary debate, it was decided that maybe a larger culvert could accommodate another Hurricane Carol, and Moulton Ridge Road would be safe from destruction forever. I might add that the worthy debate caused the closure of Moulton Ridge Road for a period of months. But we eventually got our new culvert, and it was a beauty. Its bulging, galvanized steel corrugations were covered with a thick tar on the outside and gleamed like a candidate's smile inside. It was the envy of the residents of Kensington who didn't live on Moulton Ridge Road and the pride of all of us who did. We could walk tall when entering Ester Warner's store to buy grain, gasoline, or a candy bar. We had a new culvert!

At eight years old, in 1954, I could walk tall through the new culvert; it was so big. And some forty years later, a big yellow dog figured out that she too could walk through the culvert without interference or discomfort caused by an overly expensive, but in Maggie's case, totally ineffectual, invisible fence. How she discovered that the fence was as useless as paint on a tractor, I'll never know, but she used the culvert like a highway to glory, or in her case, a highway to wherever she wanted to go. Same difference.

We learned of her fence-evading trick from her tracks in the snow. They led in and out of both ends of the culvert. We knew that they were her tracks; only a bear would leave a depression that big. Well, Tucker would leave as large an imprint, but he would never figure out an escape route through the culvert. Tucker would have difficulty devising an escape route off the couch if it was more complicated than sliding off. Most times of the year, the water at the culvert was only a foot or so deep, and Maggie could tiptoe through a foot of water.

In passing, I contemplated constructing some sort of grate that would prevent her from entering the culvert, but I gave that up as an idea that had more bad consequences than good. We made a show of keeping her home by leaving her collar on, but after a time, we didn't bother with that. Tucker was content inside the fence; he hadn't the courage or desire to follow Maggie, and at this stage of her life, Maggie was only visiting the immediate neighbors, so ...

VERSE 19

WE KEPT A COUPLE OF PIGS DURING THE SUMMERS. WE TOOK special pleasure in naming them. In the summer of 1988, we named our pigs Bushy and The Duke after George H.W. Bush and Michael Dukakis, the final presidential candidates of the year. We knew that one of the candidates would prevail, but we were equally as sure that neither Bushy nor The Duke would make it past Election Day in November. Another pig we named Natasha because we bought a sheep named Boris at the same time and wanted to honor Rocky and Bullwinkle, and I couldn't resist naming one Shalimar after Janet's mother's favorite perfume. We'd give her Shalimar at Christmas, so more Shalimar for the summer seemed only appropriate. Anyway, not to stray too far from the pigpen, our pigs lived in a sturdy wire cage large enough for them to move around in, with a roof at one end for some shade and a little protection from the rain. The whole affair was light enough in weight to allow me to move it every day through portions of the garden we had picked out. The pigs got a clean plot of land and a fresh bit of garden vegetables to root through and eat. We gained a fertilized and tilled piece of garden and fattened pigs that would fill our freezer in the fall. Maggie gained two friends with whom she could commune.

If you've heard or read that pigs are intelligent animals, then you've heard or read right. I'd say that they're right up there in intellect with nearly anyone in Congress, but I don't want you to get the wrong impression. Pigs are not only smart, but I've never questioned the veracity of a pig. Nor have I ever had the need to question the veracity of a pig. Our pigs were cheerful animals who danced when I sang to them (they're not as critical of my singing as our neighbors), grunted with delight when I moved their pen to a fresh garden spot each day, and stood (or lay) with conspiratorial interest with Maggie when she would visit with them—several times each day. It wasn't unusual to find Maggie lying beside the movable pig-pen, with the pigs lying on the inside, either sleeping or gazing across the farm with all the affinity of good friends.

Their fellowship reminded me of the over friendly display of a presidential candidate being invited to the speaker's platform and all the glad-handing that accompanies it. There's a lot of man hugging—Maggie and the pigs didn't hug—always accompanied by that maneuver where one of the man huggers, the hugger, points into the crowd and brings to the attention of the other man, the huggee, someone out there whom they both know. We have no idea what one man hugger, the pointer, is saying to the other until our last president, W, was overheard telling his future vice president what an XXXX the pointee was. Just a few simple rules about huggers and huggees. A hugger can be a pointer, and a huggee can be a pointer, but under no circumstances can a pointee be a hugger or a huggee. It just isn't done.

The introduction of the candidate has one common denominator; he or she is almost always introduced as "the next president of the United States!" In the reasonably long history of our republic, we have had forty-five presidents— forty-three presidents if you count Grover Cleveland only once. He was both the twenty-second and twenty-fourth president. Anyway, let's count Grover twice—he deserves it—and state that there are forty-five presidents but possibly thousands of next presidents. There have been Republican next presidents, Democratic next presidents, independent next presidents, Whigs and Tories, conservative and liberal, Socialist and Libertarian, even John Birchers, all presented as "the next president of the United States!"

I never saw Maggie and the pigs pointing out other animals in the crowd. "See that chicken over there? Good friend of mine! Marvelous eggs! You should steal them sometime!" My point is that Maggie and the pigs had a familial relationship. When in each other's company, they were always quiet yet attentive to each other. Usually they would touch noses in greeting through the large square holes in the fence wire and give each other a good sniff to be certain that the dog was the same dog as yesterday's dog and that the pigs didn't get swapped out during the night or traded to New York for a new pig or a pig to be named later. Of course, in spite of this warm friendship, Maggie would eat a slice of bacon with all the enthusiasm of a candidate with a fat-cat cash donor.

Though they aren't related to Maggie's story and I can't think of an appropriate way to interject them into her story, I'm compelled to say something about political advertising signs. It's okay to let people know that you're in business. The CIA conducts their business clandestinely, but just about everyone else wants you to know what they're doing, and a few signs here and there is an excellent way to tell people. TV advertising is also very effective. But political advertising is to publicity what the demolition derby is to driver training. The brightly colored signs—all of them are a very patriotic red, white, and blue—are slapped and dashed at every intersection on Route 150 with all the order of a food fight and about as welcome as weeds in a bean field. If name recognition is the attempt, then name detestation is the result. I try to make my presidential choice based on facts in evidence, but as often, I make my choice based on the candidate with the least number of signs and TV commercials. I figure that if they're smart enough to get their point across with the least number of in-your-face ads, then they're the one for me.

VERSE 20

I RECALL AN AUGUST NIGHT THAT WAS AS STILL AS THE DEW on the grass as the three of us, Janet, Maggie, and I, lay between the rows of blueberries, listening to the slight rustling of the corn and the soft, endless chirp of peepers from the trees, enjoying the sweet, familiar smell of the ripe berries, mesmerized by the grandeur of the Perseid meteor shower. Fresh from chasing frogs in the swamp, Maggie fitted herself between us, her muddy feet and fur still dripping of swamp water, soiling and soaking our clothes. We formed a quiet montage, two humans lying on our backs, watching the small bits of burning interplanetary debris streak across the sky, nearly as fast as lightning, and the dripping dog lying between us, also looking out into the universe. I noticed her steady gaze in the reflection of starlight and had the thought that Maggie had done this before, maybe every night. I don't know that she shared human understanding of our insignificance within the void, but there was more going on in that canine brain than just the prospect of the next meal. There was a sense of purpose in those soft eyes, and more than that, there was a degree of wonder. I think she experienced more than existence; she experienced being, belonging to her surroundings.

Maggie had a thoughtful side to her personality. Dogs live

in the moment, with no consideration of the future or the past, but Maggie had a pensive look at times, as though there was a thought, like another adventure, just over the hill. Life to her was more than the hour-by-hour and day-by-day undertaking of woodchucks and raccoons, neighbors and food, runners and bicycles, and, yes, police chiefs that comprise the daylight and darkness of an animal's awareness. Maggie experienced some of the nuance of being. She felt a member of the whole—a leaf on the tree of existence, contemplating the why and wherefore of the other leaves. She was as far removed from reading Nietzsche as every other dog on the block, but that didn't keep her from having a kinship with her surroundings. Some of this bond showed in her sense of humor. Yes, sense of humor that expressed itself in her games. Not chase your tail or chase the bicycle (Tucker's favorite). Actually, it was beneath her to chase anything except maybe a woodchuck or raccoon. If you threw a ball or Frisbee, she might watch it sail away, but more likely, she'd turn and expectantly watch the thrower to see how you were going to solve the problem of getting the ball/Frisbee/object back. Her games were like a candidate's talking points, devised to interact with her humans or part of a routine that she carried out around the farm.

One game was called Twin Maggies. I described earlier our front-porch door that closes with a simple spring. It remains closed until an animal pulls it open with their paw and slips through the opening. Most of our visitors arrive at our back door, located on the west side of our rambling farmhouse. When she was in residence, not with Chief Aquilina or a couple of towns away, busy being someone else's dog, Maggie greeted everyone who came to the farm and would walk with them to the back door. As soon as the guest, someone she knew like Howdy, or someone she didn't know like … like … I can't think of anyone she didn't know. I was going to say Jehovah's Witness, but she probably knew them. I'm getting sidetracked. As soon as the visitor arrived at the back door, there would follow an awkward dance where the large dog tried to occupy the same doorway at the same time as any number of humans. If she was discouraged or delayed from entry, she would turn and bolt as fast as she could around the outside of the house to the porch door, let herself in, in the manner I described earlier—standing on her back legs, pulling the doorknob, and dropping through the opening—and then run through the house to eagerly greet the visitor just entering through the back door. This was an application of the one dog, two vote rule. She would get some attention when our visitors arrived and again when she greeted them inside the house.

Surprised, new visitors would say, "You have two of these dogs!" We'd quickly explain that "No, one of these dogs was plenty!" but then as our guests were leaving, going out the same door by which they arrived, Maggie would reverse her route, and there would be the big yellow dog more often than not, panting and drooling on their shoes on the outside of the door. More than once, Janet and I were given the "Why don't you just tell us you have two of these dogs" look. Janet, always polite, would explain, whereas I'd just shrug.

Gather the Suet was a derivative of a treasure hunt, but one man's bird food is the neighbor dog's plunder. A staple of feeders of winter birds—to call people who feed birds *bird feeders* confuses them in my mind with the various-shaped containers that are used to hold bird feed—is the hard beef fat called suet. Suet is usually fed to birds in suet feeders, of which there are numerous styles and bright colors, ranging from a discarded onion bag to rectangular boxes made of cross-hatched wire, and they are all hung by a string or wire bail from a convenient tree or porch lintel for hungry winter birds to eat and enjoy. The small downy woodpeckers are active suet eaters. They're persistent as they hang with their backs to the ground, their red, tufted head a rapid-fire blur as they pick tiny bits of suet out from between the squares of wire or onion bag.

It's important—at least it was important for our neighbors—to hang your suet feeder quite high. Higher than, oh say, the standing reach of a big yellow dog that might be out canvassing the neighborhood for snacks as enthusiastically as a candidate gathering votes. Our front lawn blossomed with many gay-colored suet feeders that Maggie collected and carried home during the winter. She could reach higher in trees or porches as she stood on the increasing snow base, pull the feeders full of suet down, bring them home, rip them open, and empty them on our front lawn, so by spring, she had a significant assortment of feeders. As winter progressed and following snows covered the evidence, I thought little of her collections, but as the snow melted in the spring, revealing the colorful winter crop of our neighbors' suet feeders, it became a little embarrassing. Rudy or Jim Falconer or the Holmes would drive by, and I'd see them pointing at our lawn. I didn't need to read lips to understand what they were saying to the car's occupants. Every other day or so, I'd gather up the exposed feeders and discard them into the trash. Hey, I didn't know whose was which, so I couldn't very well return them, and it seemed a little crass to pile them beside the mailbox with a sign that read, "Free to a good home." That's how we got these problems in the first place.

It isn't productive to think of a dog's digestive tract, but all that suet couldn't have been good for her. Feeder following feeder of raw suet must have been like trying to digest—raw suet. I can't think of anything comparable. Maggie was always robust, energetic, and healthy, but there were days when I wondered why.

Another of her favorite games was called Bowling in the Corn. When someone was in the cornfield, picking or just inspecting—the corn had to be eight or ten feet high, nearly ripe, the rows forming a leafy green tunnel—Maggie would run at full tilt down the rows, crashing through the hanging leaves with a sound of trees whipping in a hurricane. The best part was to nearly topple the human in the corn by blasting past them in the same row and barely brushing by them. The object of the game, I believe, was to see how close she could get to the person without actually touching them. If she could make them fall, she gave herself extra points, depending upon how hard the collision. A hard collision was worth fewer extra points than a light brush by. Even Tucker could upend a two-legged being by using brute force, but the brush by delivered at top speed required style and technique. The human would think that the big yellow dog running nearly out of control would bowl them over like a spare tenpin, when in fact the big yellow dog would alter her course by inches at the last second, and the braced human would topple while trying to regain footing as the big yellow dog sped by.

Bowling in the Corn didn't require a special human. Charlie's stamina and athleticism were unnecessary. Old, Slow

Dave would do just fine, but the best humans for Bowling in the Corn were kids. They had the required spirit. Cameron liked corn. He'd often go picking with me, and Cameron liked to run, and Cameron liked the game, even adding a wrinkle or two by stepping into an adjacent row as Maggie careened by, like changing lanes on a freeway. I wasn't just Old, Slow Dave. I could be Dave born of gravity or just plain Dave the Old Grouch, and though Dave yelling "Maggie, stop it!' was great, it added a dimension of seriousness to the game, and after a half hour or so, he started to become a drag.

Corn was Maggie's favorite crop. When young, it was often cultivated, keeping the soil soft and easy to dig—a perfect place to bury treasures. A freshly killed woodchuck or new beef bone could be effortlessly buried to ripen for a few days—then exhumed to be rolled in or carried to the lawn for Janet to run over with the lawn mower. As the corn matured, it was a great hiding place. If I was looking for Maggie to take her to the vet, for example, an acre or two of tall corn waving in the breeze could provide plenty of cover to discourage a long search.

Because it grew tall like a dense forest, a field of corn held many surprises. Before maturity, it was a perfect haven for wild turkeys. The turkeys felt secure in the lush growth, and Maggie felt secure in finding them. Turkeys need a little runway to get airborne, and for a turkey to fly in tall cornstalks is a little like a small plane flying in a forest. Maggie wouldn't kill a turkey—they put up a surprising battle—but chasing them through the corn was a little like the running of the bulls in Pamplona. An observer would see a roiling mass of cornstalks, dust, and pollen swirling in the air and hear the banshee cry of thirty or so distressed turkeys running blindly through the rows, pursued by a large, deliriously happy yellow dog. I was never sure if she chased the turkeys because it was fun or if she felt that she was protecting the crop from the large birds. I don't think the turkeys ate much corn, but for the turkeys, I know that our blueberry yield would be much improved.

Raccoons were a different story. The masked marauders are as relentless as presidential candidates and do economic damage because they eat a lot of corn. Though outnumbered probably twenty to one, Maggie took raccoon duty very seriously. Raccoons are excellent judges of good, ripe sweet corn. I can tell if the corn is ready to pick by the degree of raccoon damage, and they're as hard to discourage from the corn as a child from Halloween candy. They forage in large groups called a gaze—though to call it a graze would be more accurate—and eat only the mature ears and not an ear that has an insect or a blemish in it. One August night many summers ago, soon after the introduction of the transistor radio, my sister placed a radio in a small corn crop in a field near the farmhouse. The idea was that the raccoons would hear human voices and not come near, so she found an all-night talk station and set the volume at about half register. The following morning, Betty looked to her new invention, only to find the immediate area around the radio cleared of the ears of corn and the remnant husks and cobs, eaten clean of the sweet kernels, piled delicately around the radio. The only thing missing from the party scene were empty beer bottles.

Maggie practiced a different tactic. She discouraged the raccoons by invoking the fear of God. The raccoons usually came after nightfall, which was just fine with Maggie. The night provided her greater invisibility. The yellow stealth protector of the corn would quietly enter the field, becoming no more than a shadow in the hushed dark. When she felt she could get no closer without setting off a raccoon alarm, she would charge into the group, barking, growling, snarling, and snapping, sending the entire gaze running to the nearest trees, there to spend the remaining night safe from the big yellow avenger. Maggie prowled around the base of the trees until she was bored with the whole venture. Then she'd splash into the brook to cool off before trotting down to Route 150, looking for Chief Aquilina, or joining me on the couch for a little TV, maybe a ball game, before retiring. The raccoons usually took a few nights off before trying the corn and Maggie's assault again.

The raccoons would be a little put out if they understood one of the reasons Maggie protected the corn. One look at Maggie's stools in late summer, and you'd understand that sweet corn was at least a minor part of her diet. Yes, the fox was guarding the henhouse, so to speak. Or like Congressman Wilbur Mills watched Fanne Fox in the tidal basin, Maggie really liked corn, though she didn't pick it off the stalks; she waited for me to give her an ear, shared the pig's supply of day-old corn, or ate the raccoons' leavings. She'd comfortably lie down and hold the ear upright like an ice-cream cone between her front paws and chew away happily, with stray kernels sticking to her lips and muzzle in a yellow froth.

Maggie and the raccoons had a number of things in common. They enjoyed chicken, eggs, and corn, though Maggie's taste for chicken ran more in the roasted or deep-fried leftovers as she matured. But she would always be the dirty old egg-sucking hound of country music fame. I tried explaining to her the presence of salmonella in raw eggs, but it fell on deaf ears. I think her attitude was *what's good enough for the raccoons is good enough for me.* Maybe by eating so many eggs, she thought she was protecting Janet and me from the perils of salmonella.

At the end of corn season, we harrow the cornstalks and any remaining ears into the soil and plant a crop of winter rye to hold and feed the soil until spring, and that's when, like the brides at Macy's, the Canada Geese arrive. They forage through the leavings and feed on stray kernels and chaff in great numbers. There may be more than fifty geese in the field as they take a day off from their migration south for a little corn shopping. When she was young, Maggie would chase the geese, or attempt to chase the geese, out of the field, but the birds would lift themselves a short distance into the air on their powerful wings, hover overhead, and voice their displeasure with a discordant chorus of honks and squeals until the bothersome dog was gone, then alight on the ground for a little more foraging.

With age, Maggie learned that chasing geese was as productive as getting a ride home with Chef Aquilina—he didn't care anymore—so she just joined them in their rummaging for food. Good concierge that she was, she mingled with the geese, certain that they had a good thing going with this leftover corn shopping, although to put it without delicacy, she may have been more interested in goose poop than old corn. Dogs have a strange taste for what tastes strange.

VERSE LAST

ALL GOOD THINGS MUST COME TO AN END. THAT'S TRUE OF presidential campaigns, growing seasons, and the life of a dog. We can predict the ending, though in the case of a campaign, we know that it will end, we just don't know until the end what the outcome will be. Every growing season concludes with the initial hard frost, and we know from the first moment that our pets are with us that a day will arrive when they will go on to a greater reward and we will remain behind to reason our way through the labyrinth of sadness. So it was with Maggie. I came into the kitchen one late summer morning, expecting to find nothing more incriminating than the evidence of some food left inadvertently on the counter from the night before, maybe a shredded cereal box or bread wrapper from one of the kids' late-night snack. Instead, Maggie's lifeless body was lying beside the dog's water bowl; she had taken a drink, lay down on the floor, and life left her. She appeared no different than she did in life, her face and powerful body relaxed and comfortable, her long legs extended where she lay down on her side, and soil from the garden still clinging to her huge feet from what must have been her last romp with the raccoons in the corn.

My first thought when I saw her was of disbelief. That a body with so much life could be so suddenly an empty shell was beyond reason. I touched her as I would a sleeping child, not wanting to wake her, just wanting to assure myself that it was sleep that separated her from the living, knowing that it was a more eternal state. Maggie, in her life, had presented us with every expectation, from wander to wonder, from laughter to love, but never the thought of death. She was always too alive.

We have an animal burial ground on the farm. A place set aside, surrounded by quiet green lawn, only disturbed by the occasional trespass of the lawn mower. Maggie rests there, within sight of the cornfield.

EPILOGUE

Postscript—October 2015

MANY YEARS, TEARS, AND MUCH JOY HAS BEEN VISITED UPON us since Maggie left. A few more dogs have shared and improved our lives and passed on to whatever it is we pass on to. I'm sure it's joyful. Mocha, a gentle giant, was a sweet, quiet Great Pyrenees, a genteel reflection of Tucker. The two big white dogs, inseparable over time, became a landmark of sorts, posed on the front lawn together, their size and color an easily recognized point of reference. "Just drive up Moulton Ridge Road. The Lambert farm is the one with the two white dogs on the lawn. You can't miss it."

When Janet's brother, Buck, Maggie's good friend and our colossus who rode the strawberry planter, passed from this world, he rewarded and entrusted us with Sadie. She was an older mixed breed (maybe pit bull, maybe terrier, maybe tick hound), who traveled with Janet and me on our twelve-thousand-mile odyssey across America and back, a wonderful experience for us and I think for Sadie, regaled in her regal ermine collar, ruler of all she surveyed.

The big, old farmhouse echoes with a hollower sound these days as Janet and I share it with no one. The dogs are gone, and the cats are gone, all having lived a long, healthy life, and as we approach another crossroad in our lives, we choose not to replace them. They thrived in an agrarian world that no longer exists. In my lifetime, a dozen or more farms in Kensington have converted from agriculture to architecture. The main crops were food and fodder; now it's McMansions and McPeople. There is an enforced leash law. Our animals could have adapted to a different environment, but they wouldn't have been who they were, and neither would we. Life is the sum of our experiences, a tally of all we see, hear, and do, and we shouldn't want to change it if we could. We should do our best to get it right the first time.

Our presidential primary is still with us; however, in this domain, there is little change. There is, this year, a stampede of presidential prospects invading our quiet state. I dare not go to town for fear of being accosted for my vote. Bombast and promises have reached an epic high. Each contestant has a different plan for improving our lives. While one will lower my taxes a little, another will lower my taxes quite a bit, and yet another will lower my taxes to almost nothing. I listened so hard that I got a headache, yet I heard not one say that my taxes would go up, though we know that there will be an increase; it's inevitable.

Some will stop the war, some will slow down the war, and one said that he would start a war that he would then stop or slow down. When someone asked which war it was he wanted to stop, he replied by saying that he would be sure that our taxes went down.

They all agree that Washington is a den of vipers, a jungle alive with lobbyists and members of Congress and that they, most of whom are members of Congress, are the individual best suited to drain the swamp. It's a weird and perverse form of entertainment, just watching and listening, but as a friend of mine said last week, it's cheaper than going to the movies.

I'm keeping my vote for the candidate who will give me new tires for my tractor. I don't know who he is yet, but I'm certain that he, or of course she, will present themselves.

I'm told that I should not go up and down stairs anymore, and to accomplish that, we moved our bedroom downstairs to the living room and remodeled the downstairs bath and put in a shower worthy of a senator. I was going to stay worthy of a king, but of course, we don't have a king, so I went to the next most opulent individual of whom I could think.

A reader will find it boring if I go on about brass fixtures and a vessel bowl sink, so I won't go on about them. Now, it came to pass that in this fine remodeled bathroom, we installed a white pine floor.

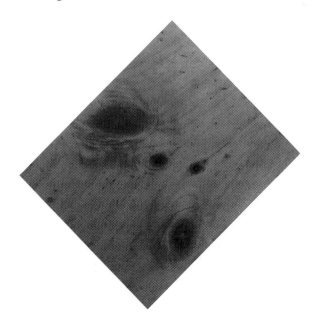

When the floor was sanded and polished to perfection, the surface gleaming with many coats of urethane, I entered the room, looked down at the floor, and froze midstride. There, formed by a random collection of knots and swirls, highlighted by the glossy urethane finish, was the exact image of Maggie. I should say all the Maggies. Not the first-day Maggie or the last-day Maggie but Maggie of all her days. Her ears perked, her muzzle tense, her eyes as round, bright, and expectant as black jewels. The perfect "What do you say, Dave? Want to take a swim in the pond and then go find Chief Aquilina?"

ABOUT THE AUTHOR

DAVID LAMBERT WAS BORN IN 1942 IN NORWICH, Connecticut. At the start of WW2, his father found work at the Portsmouth Naval Shipyard, and the family moved to Kittery, Maine. At war's end, they bought the small farm on Moulton Ridge Road in Kensington, New Hampshire, and except for an enlistment in the Marine Corps after high school, David didn't leave Moulton Ridge Road for seventy years; but for stairs and Parkinson's disease, he would live there still. "Surrounded by dogs, loving family, and old farm machines, could life have been any better?"

ABOUT THE ILLUSTRATOR

C. HOFFMAN WAS BORN IN 1999 IN BRENTWOOD, NEW Hampshire, and it was to the great joy of the grandparents that the illustrator spent so many early years at their farm— the farm in our story. The artist's innate ability and imagination were refined at Granite State Arts Academy, where they graduated in 2018. The energy that emerges from the images gives testimony to the warmth and love of the farm that was acquired early in life.

C. Hoffman is the enduring grandchild of the author.